SEABIRDS

An Unofficial Illustrated Encyclopedia of Naval Aviation

Aerocatures ™ and Text
by Hank Caruso

Designed by Lotta Helleberg
Edited by Katherine A. Neale and Ross A. Howell, Jr.

Library of Congress Catalog Card Number 95-80601
ISBN 1-57427-046-X

Printed in Hong Kong

Published by Howell Press, Inc.,
1147 River Road, Suite 2
Charlottesville, Virginia 22901
Telephone (804) 977-4006

First Printing

HOWELL PRESS

FOREWORD

Without a doubt, the greatest high achieved by this Naval Aviator was not the excitement of going Mach 2 in the A-5A (A3J-1) Vigilante, engaging in combat in the A-6A Intruder, assuming squadron command, or even serving as the commanding officer of the great aircraft carrier *Coral Sea.* Rather, it was being able to experience the camaraderie that goes with squadron and shipboard life.

Tailhookers come from all over our great country . . . north, south, east, west, inner city, farm, and mountains. They represent all ethnic backgrounds and social strata. They earn their wings of gold, survive nugget life, and become salts in one short cruise. Continually pushing themselves to the limit, they become the cutting edge of American foreign policy when the question "Where are the carriers?" is asked. Associating with these young, bright, courageous, eager, hard-charging warriors on a daily basis remains, to this day, my own personal high.

Naval Aviators push the edge of the envelope each and every time they strap on an aircraft and take it flying. Hank Caruso captures that spirit, that moment of truth, that in-your-face attitude that separates the warrior from all others. From his fertile mind and through his sharp pen, Hank gives the aircraft and carriers he draws the emotions Naval Aviators experience as they live carrier aviation: from the thrill of the cat shot and the awesome feeling of accomplishment when missiles hit tail pipes and bombs obliterate targets, to the terror of the pitching deck night recovery. Hank captures it all!

Dick Dunleavy
Vice Admiral, U.S. Navy (Retired)

3

INTRODUCTION

There are many ways to depict Naval Aviation. Some excellent motion pictures and documentaries have appeared in the past fifty years, from William Wyler's World War II documentary *The Fighting Lady* to *The Bridges at Toko-ri* of Korean War fame, to the more recent Vietnam War saga, *Flight of the Intruder*. Magazines such as *The Hook, Naval Aviation News*, and *Wings of Gold* describe carrier aviation past and present. The Naval Aviation Museum's quarterly publication, *Foundation*, is rich in first-person accounts. Additionally, Naval Aviation has been blessed with the talents of photographers such as the legendary Edward Steichen. More recently, Bob Lawson, Harry Gann, and Tom Twomey have added to our visual knowledge and pleasure.

Some of us devote our energies to researching and writing about Naval Aviation's exciting past and its contributions to American freedom and the aeronautical sciences. Colleagues such as John Lundstrom, Zip Rausa, and Jack Elliot specialize in this rewarding facet of aviation history.

Among aviation artists, the decades-long contributions of R.G. Smith and Ted Wilbur have set a very high standard. Cartoonists have found fertile ground in Naval Aviation as well. The Navy's first official aviation cartoonist was the late Robert Osborne, famous for his series of World War II training posters featuring Dilbert, the thick-headed aviator, and Spoiler, the dim-witted mechanic.

But Hank Caruso's niche is unique, an approach entirely his own. Aside from his distinctive drafting style, he has become accepted as *the* caricaturist of Navy air. At first glance, his renditions are delightfully outlandish. But on second look — and third and fourth — his Seabirds possess the unmistakable ring of truth.

This is no accident. Hank depicts his subjects so well because he's been there and done that. I met him about a decade ago at Tailhook '80-something, and soon realized why he's so successful. Only someone who has experienced the fearsome four rides in the helo dunker can fully appreciate the mixture of truth and humor in his rendition of a submerged exit from a sunken helicopter trainer. Only someone who's grunted through high-G maneuvers, trying to maintain eye contact with the bogey in an ACM (air combat maneuvering) hop, will smile a knowing grin at the progressively sagging facial muscles. And for tailhookers, only those who have hit the boat can fully appreciate the subtleties of Hank's interpretation of T-2s during carrier qualifications, as the now-retired *Lexington* launches her birds with a slingshot, a ready-deck catcher's mitt on the stern.

Therefore, I'm pleased to flash two thumbs up and to log an OK-3 for Hank Caruso's SEABIRDS, the book. The only thing possibly better in this day of sophisticated animation would be *Seabirds*, the movie. When that bright day dawns, I'll be first in line to buy a ticket.

Barrett Tillman
Aviation Author and Historian

IN THE BEGINNING...

My first exposure to the world of aviation was as a four-month-old infant in 1945, flying on a DC-3 with my parents from my birthplace of Fort Benning, Georgia, to our new home in Connecticut. My dad enjoyed telling me how on that flight I threw up all over his uniform. Thus, at a very early age, flying and motion sickness became inextricably inter-twined in my life.

Throughout my childhood, I was hopelessly entranced by anything that flew, whether natural or man-made. (In my art, I've always used birds or bird-like creatures as alter egos.) Fortunately for me, the late 1940s and 1950s were the *real* golden age of aviation. New propulsion systems and materials made all the old rules of physics obsolete and opened flight envelopes to unheard-of speeds and altitudes. Dozens of aircraft manufac-turers (compared to the handful that now remains) developed literally hundreds of kerosene-propelled aluminum test tubes to rewrite the rule books defining the games humans play with flying machines. Best of all, the public's intense fascination with new technology in general, and avia-tion in particular, ensured that we airplane groupies could indulge our-selves in an extravaganza of entertainment and news media coverage of every aeronautical subject imaginable.

That new monochrome wonder of technology, television, was a logical home for tales of aviation excitement. Thousands of small black-and-white screens became as wide as the heavens with series such as *Steve Canyon, The Blue Angels, Navy Log, Whirlybirds, The Man and the Challenge, Men In Space*, and the superb *Air Power* series. On Saturday mornings, Hollywood stars shared top billing with high-tech flying machines on bigger screens at local theaters. Feature attractions included *Jet Pilot, Men of the Fighting Lady, The Bridges at Toko-ri, Strategic Air Command, Bombers B-52, The McConnell Story*, and the Holy Grail of '50s aviation cinema, *Toward the Unknown*.

Powerhouse magazines such as *Life, Colliers, Look*, and *National Geographic* regularly featured aviation developments, real and specula-tive, often illustrated with superbly evocative paintings by the nation's leading aviation and space artists. Plastic model kits from Revell, Aurora, and Lindbergh boasted box art with dubious technical accuracy, but enor-mous emotional appeal. Millions of gallons of jet fuel were converted to soul-satisfying decibels every year above insatiable airshow audiences at air bases that never seemed to be too far from home. Cardboard cutout models of such modern aviation wonders as the F-94 and 707 were even featured on the backs of Cheerios cereal boxes. A genuine spirit of excitement about aviation advances was an inseparable part of the culture in which I grew up.

The public relations department at every aircraft manufacturer seemed to have a staff set aside just to handle requests for pictures from adolescent airplane junkies. Not only did they *always* respond to our requests, but most actually had budget money set aside to develop and print special photos, paintings, and booklets specifically for kids, kids who bought no products, owned no shares, signed no contracts, and brought in no customers . . . a truly unthinkable frivolity in today's aero-space industry.

I received a pretty piddling allowance as a kid, but even as far back as fourth grade I saved whatever money I could to buy postcards. Postcards were magic parchments to be inscribed with the words that would cajole public relations departments out of whatever treasures I could. I reasoned that a typed request would look more official (important people always corresponded with typed postcards) and therefore earn the greater rewards that were due the inner circle. As a result, my typing skills developed at a very early age.

My peers and I competed to find the best sources of airplane loot. I haunted the public library and religiously researched each issue of *Aviation Week* for the names and addresses of likely sources of promotional treasure. Whenever one of us struck a mother lode, he would gloatingly display his newly acquired riches, while keeping their source the blackest of secrets. We jealously cut the return addresses from envelopes and hid the valuable scraps so that no other treasure hunter could share in the wealth.

I still have all the aviation material that I was so fortunate to acquire decades ago. The pictures, pamphlets, and paintings never fail to evoke the same wonderful spirit of adventure and limitless possibility, the naive excitement of aviation pioneering, that I felt when I was growing up. The passion that those marketeers had for what they did is almost completely unknown now, but it still shows in the memorabilia that they created for us. I will always be indebted to all those nameless people who made the reality of aviation so magically accessible to me in that golden age of promotional passion and enthusiasm.

Connecticut had a healthy aerospace industry in the 1950s, but there were no convenient hotbeds of aviation activity to visit on a regular basis. The closest was Brainard Field, where my parents would drive me whenever I could persuade them to watch what little general aviation and commercial air traffic there was. Later, my friends and I would bicycle there from my home in Wethersfield and wander among private aircraft tied down at the flight line, sneaking peeks into the cockpits. A general aviation field at the time, it still showed fascinating vestiges of earlier glories. I remember in particular that on the floor of what must have once been the passenger terminal was an elaborate inlaid compass. I often looked at that floor and tried to imagine what sort of operation this might have been twenty years earlier.

Bradley Field in Windsor Locks was the next best opportunity to get close to the real world of aviation. A seemingly short trip in terms of miles, the road infrastructure at the time meant that my parents and I were in for a day-long trek. I spent many hours on the observation deck there with my plastic box camera, waiting for just the right moment to snap the picture, that moment when an airliner would just begin to turn over its engines on a cold day, expelling a dramatic puff of white smoke and condensation. After pushing my family's endurance to the limit on the observation deck, I would cruise up and down the main aisle of the passenger terminal collecting postcards, literature, and decals from the different airline counters. The stickers all went on the headboard of my bed.

Probably the most memorable of my visits to Bradley Field was the introduction of the Boeing 707 to the airways. A special viewing was held for the public, which we went to one night. The magical interior of the aircraft was also available for viewing. The sight of that incredible example of the aerodynamicist's art at night, dramatically highlighted by spotlights, was like being part of a real-life science fiction epic.

Springfield, Massachusetts, was the home of Westover Air Force Base and the Eastern States Exposition. The Eastern States Exposition was a yearly event on a scale the likes of which disappeared decades ago. There were displays from every imaginable business and manufacturer, as well as the military services. The highlight was an airshow that included flybys of the most advanced Air Force inventory and a demonstration by the Thunderbirds in their beautiful North American F-100s. Westover AFB was home to the new, truly awesome Boeing B-52 Stratofortress. Flight line displays included all the pre-Century-series fighters, including my favorite, the Northrop F-89 Scorpion. (This is the first airplane on which I can remember seeing a face.) These experiences fueled something very deep inside me.

I think in the back of my head I always saw the Air Force as the place where the action was. But my eyesight was terrible. There was no way that I could ever be a front-seater with eyeglasses . . . and if I couldn't be a pilot, what was the point? The only backseaters I knew about were navigators and navigation involved lots of math. I did pretty well in math throughout my school years, but couldn't envision a career based on manipulating numbers. I've never seen myself as a mechanic. And the thought of a life of staying indoors dealing with paperwork (which I now do most of the time) had little appeal. As for the Navy, it involved lots of very deep water in which one could drown. Certainly not the place I wanted to be.

When I graduated with my bachelor's degree in mechanical engineering from Cornell University, the Vietnam War was in full swing. I followed the events, the Johnson administration's micromanagement of the conflict, and the air community's frustrations in *Aviation Week*. My college occupation as a mechanical engineer was considered valuable to the national interest, so I was granted a defense deferment. This status continued when I took a job at Westinghouse Electric Corporation as an environmental simulation engineer. I worked on developing fire control radars for the C, D, and E versions of the F-4 Phantom II, electronic countermeasures (including the jamming system for the F-105G Wild Weasel), and other military avionics that were giving American warriors a small advantage during this unfortunate conflict. I know that I made a more useful contribution to the war effort by using my engineering talents in a test laboratory than I could have by pushing papers or slinging a rifle. Still, a part of me feels that I missed something very important by not pursuing a career in military aviation. There is an energy, a spirit of dedication and trust, and a satisfying sense of purpose and idealism in the military aviation community that I have never found in the civilian world.

The Story Behind Seabirds

My first contact with the Naval Aviation community was in 1980 when a friend in marketing communications showed my artwork to the editor of *Naval Aviation News*, renowned aviation artist, Capt. Ted Wilbur, USN (Ret.). Shortly thereafter, my first minigallery appeared in the March 1981 issue along with the term that I coined for my aviation caricatures: Aerocatures™. However, I could not figure out how to depict the actual Naval aviators themselves. I could base images of Air Force aviators on aircraft nicknames: Eagles (F-15), Warthogs (a.k.a. Horatio Hogbreath for the A-10), Rhinos (F-4), and Vipers (F-16). These very distinctive animal images were all tied together by a consistency of personality and attitude that was pretty easy to translate into a visual cast of characters.

On the other hand, the nicknames for Navy aircraft were a mixed bag of inconsistent images: the F-18 Hornet (I don't like bugs), the F-14 Tomcat (Grumman's superb twin-tailed cat cartoon was someone else's idea), the F-4 Phantom, the A-6 Intruder (How do you draw an intruder?), the A-7 Corsair, and so on. Since I could find no common ground for an image based on aircraft names, I adopted a more generic approach. I began with a large-beaked, well-muscled, aggressive-looking bird and added a strap-on tailhook to symbolize Naval Aviation: the Seabird. The first Seabirds made their debut in the February 1982 issue of *Naval Aviation News*. Since then, they have made numerous appearances as pilots, NFOs, aircrew, carrier deck crew, mechanics and technicians, physiologists, parachute riggers, and engineers.

Seabirds are very versatile images. They straddle the visual border between aircraft and aviator. Their beaks and wings can represent either human features or aircraft structures. I use their beaks as devices to reflect the particular role I'm trying to depict: beaks for the aviators might have "No Step" stenciling, flight sensors, antennas, camouflage patterns, or kill markings; mechanics might have beaks with access panels or electrical connectors; engineers' beaks come equipped with pocket protectors, instruments, data readouts, and clipboards. With the right props (flight suit, tailhook, coveralls, oversize oxygen mask, rotor backpack, and so on) — and Naval Aviation is nothing if not laden with props — Seabirds can represent any role in Naval Aviation.

Where Do the Ideas Come From?

People invariably ask me how I get my ideas. The answer I give is that this is the way I see things. I know that's not a very satisfying answer; it's not meant to be dismissive. It's just that I don't know any other way to describe what happens in my head. I generally cannot work at creating an idea; it either pops up with a life of its own or it doesn't. As far as I can remember, I have always seen faces on airplanes. No, not just faces, personalities. Each airplane has its own distinct personality. Growing up, I was frustrated that I couldn't explain this to others . . . at least not with words, which was my only vocabulary at the time.

Aerocatures™ are the language I did not have as a kid, the vocabulary that finally let me share my visions with others. For me, aircraft are more than mere mechanical contrivances. They are the ultimate expression of their creators' visions, the personalities of their pilots and crews. Aircraft were my connection with the power and excitement of what people can do and become. They have personality, spirit, and attitude.

I don't see myself as a cartoonist. I view my art as portraits of how man-made objects, physical forces, and human feelings come together and interact. I want to capture the feelings that define the whole aviation experience, not just the outlines of the airplanes. That's why I strive for realism — in addition to technical accuracy — in the situations I portray. I want to tell a complete and believable story. This is the way I talk to people, the way I share ideas and visions. After my childhood communication frustrations, my greatest personal satisfaction is when an aviator shows my drawings to a child or a friend and says, "See, this is what it feels like, this is what I do, this is who I am."

I am a self-taught artist. My only formal art training came from my college mechanical drafting courses, which gave me the essentials of perspective, spatial relations, and three-dimensional structures. As a kid, I preferred pencils and crayons to paints. Paints were always just beyond my grasp as a medium and generally ended up as a brown syrup on the canvas. Perhaps part of the problem was that I saw (and still see) things in terms of line and contour rather than color.

My early coloring books show that my first step with each picture was to redraw the printed outlines with a black crayon before proceeding to fill in the outlines with color. Today, I use the same technique, although not quite with such a heavy hand. I fill in my outlines with shading or color. The line work is done with mechanical drafting pens; the color is done with Prismacolor® colored pencils. These pencils lay down layers of color that can be blended by using some of the lighter colors. This hides the pencil strokes and makes it difficult for those not familiar with this medium to figure out just how the illustration was done. The only drawback to working with these media is that it is very time-consuming to cover large areas with fine-line cross-hatching and pencil points. As a result, I typically work in smaller sizes (11" x 14" to 14" x 22") than most painters.

Each Aerocature™ comes to life by bouncing back and forth between my right and left brain. The process always starts with the intuitive inspiration of the right brain. I cannot begin a drawing by looking at a photograph. This is a left-brain process and results in a drawing that looks like a bad copy of the original. Instead, I have to work from my stored impressions of the subject and how I want the whole picture to feel. At this point, accuracy is a distraction.

Once I have the feeling right on my sketch pad, I transfer the image lightly in pencil to smooth-surface Bristol drawing paper. Now I can switch over to the left brain and consult my reference sources to get the details right. Sometimes this involves recomposing the entire image, but I generally manage to preserve the spirit of the original sketch. With the initial outlines complete, I bounce back to the right brain so that I can use fine-line shading to establish surface contours, textures, and all those other characteristics that add feeling and atmosphere to the illustration.

The bottom line is that I can't do a good job of drawing anything that I don't understand at a gut level. For me, research goes beyond collecting airplane pictures and books. I like to be alone with an aircraft so I can get to know it intimately. I especially enjoy being around an airplane at night when no one else is near, in a boneyard communing with aircraft awaiting restoration or the scrap blade, or being in hangars with aircraft that are torn down for repair or maintenance. These are times when I learn much more about my subjects than I can in a crowd or from a sterile reference source.

I try to imagine what it was like to be the designer, to appreciate his style and attitude, to understand why he shaped each feature, curve, bump, or bulge the way he did; why things are placed where they are and what they do; how the airplane feels when lifting forces bend its wings up

or gravity bends its fuselage down; what kind of attitude goes with its mission. I want to get to know it through the viewfinder of my cameras, to have it pose for me, to understand how it looks the same and different from each new angle. And I want to touch it, to run my hands over its different surfaces and feel their smoothness, hardness, or curvature, to sense the thickness or compliance of its skin and the nature of the structure underneath.

Another resource that I draw on is my interest in all manner of three-dimensional publications and presentations. As far back as grade school, I drew pictures that had objects flying out of the picture plane and extending past the limits of the background. This style is something that I still use today; it has become one of the defining characteristics of Aerocatures™. Whether I'm drawing or viewing, I like the experience of that third dimension, images that draw me into them and make me feel as though I'm part of what I'm viewing. When it comes to portraying aviation, two dimensions just aren't enough.

Understanding the aircraft is only the beginning. My research also includes the human side of aviation. I talk to pilots, other crew members, ground and support personnel. I want to know why they do what they do, what gets them excited, what scares them, how they feel about their squadron mates. Becoming a fly on the wall and listening to conversations in officer's and enlisted personnel club bars or ready rooms, attending briefings and debriefings, and having one-on-one discussions with the crews is the starting point. Eventually, though, nothing substitutes for actually being in the cockpit, maneuvering, pulling Gs, feeling the exhilaration and the discomfort, or watching deck or ground crews work. This firsthand experience is what the Navy has given me.

After undergoing survival and physiology training, including the ejection seat trainer, altitude chamber, and swim test in full flight gear, I earned the privilege of flying in the backseats of many Navy tactical jet, propeller, and rotary wing aircraft. These flights include hops with the Navy's Fighter Weapons School (Top Gun), Blue Angels, and US Naval Test Pilot School, along with cruises on board several different aircraft carriers. These experiences have given me a perspective that I would never have had as an outside spectator. Words and photographs in reference books cannot substitute for being there. Often I can't point to any specific drawing and identify what feature would have been different had I not had these experiences, but I do know that these firsthand experiences have had a profound cumulative influence on the character and authenticity of what I illustrate. So whether I am drawing Seabirds or caricatures of the aircraft themselves, I am better able to make them strong and human and, most importantly, real.

Ultimately, I want to share my ideas and experiences at several different levels. After the initial visual impact, I want to leave more subtle messages to look for, insider jokes that only a few might appreciate (such as my initials hidden somewhere in each drawing). By paying attention to detail and letting myself have fun with my ideas, I want to invite my audience to become more personally involved by making their own discoveries. In some cases, they will find messages and meanings that I was not aware of when I created the drawings. Other times, they will focus on a particular detail that triggers very personal reactions for them based on their individual experiences. When this happens, I feel like I've communicated with others in a way I never could as a child.

Hank Caruso

A Personal Dedication

This book is more than a collection of artwork. It is a personal thank-you to all the Navy and Marine officers and enlisted personnel who have been so generous with their time and trust. They have shared with me their intense dedication, excitement, and disappointments, achievements and personal losses. I have been privileged to see the loyalty that all of them bear towards their comrades, their chosen service, and the country they are sworn to defend, a loyalty they maintain even when unjustly maligned by the media or indifferently abandoned to the short-sighted selfishness of political correctness and administrative convenience.

A special attitude and spirit go with Naval Aviation that I hope I've captured successfully. These are important things that deserve to be appreciated and preserved. Indeed, they must be preserved if the military that we expect to defend this country is to remain viable and credible. Unhappily, the trend of recent events threatens to place this spirit in jeopardy. SEABIRDS is dedicated to celebrating and preserving the spirit of Naval Aviation in the hopes that what I've been privileged to see and experience will still be there for others to appreciate and be a part of in the future.

For those of you who have helped me experience the story of Naval Aviation over the past dozen years, please know how deeply grateful I am for your gifts of knowledge and trust. For those of you whom my records failed to include, who were filed in brain cells that have long since died, or who I never knew were there, my apologies, but my gratitude all the same. (The ranks of officers listed reflect when I worked with them last. Many have since been promoted or retired.)

My thanks to: LCdr. Ralph Alderson, LCdr. C.L. Anderson, Cdr. Trish Beckman, LCdr. Chris Benjes, Heidi Benson, Cdr. Tom Bernsen, RAdm. Pete Booth, Ken Bushpics, Capt. Ken Carlton, LCdr. Ward Carroll, the late Cdr. Bob Christensen, Chris Cikanovich, Lt. Lisa Curtin, LCdr. Rod Davis, Cdr. Mike Denkler, LCdr. Steve Dole, Capt. Dan Driscoll (USMC), Capt. Ray Dudderar, VAdm. Dick Dunleavy, Sandy Dyson, Mike Eide, LCdr. Robin Erichsen, Keith Ferris, Lt. John Foley, Lt. Lee Grawn, PR1 J. Harwood, Lt. Carol Reinbird (Hassan), Capt. Bill Hayden, Randy Hepp, Lisa Hudgins, Jan Jacobs, Cdr. Bert Johnston, Cdr. Russ Jowers, Cdr. John Keilty, Capt. Dick Knott, LCdr. Michael Krechel, Capt. James Lair, LCdr. Tom Linthicum, LCdr. Barry Love, Cdr. Rick Ludwig, LCdr. Doug McClain, Steve Millikin, Cdr. Pat Moneymaker, LCdr. Huck Morgan, LCdr. Gray Morrison, Cdr. John Norton, Capt. Jeff Olsen (USMC), Cdr. Tom Otterbein, Lt. Dave Parsons, Denis Powers, LtCol. Bob Price (USMC), Vern Pugh, Capt. Zip Rausa, Bill Readdy, Cdr. Dusty Rhoades, LCdr. Mike Rohman, LCdr. Kent Rominger, Sandy Russell, Eric Ryberg, Cdr. Dan Shewell, LCdr. Terry Shoemaker, Dave Short, Lt. (jg) L.D. Smith, R.G. Smith, Cdr. Tom Sobiek, RAdm. George Strohsahl Jr., Ron Thomas, Barrett Tillman, Capt. Vance Toalson, LCdr. Liz Toedt, LCdr. Dave Vail and Mary Vail, Capt. Phil Voss, LCdr. Curt Watson, Cdr. Howie Wheeler, Capt. Ted Wilbur (Ret.), Cdr. Bob Williams, and Lt. Sandy Winnefeld.

The Stick

When VAQ-141 asked me to develop a portrait of the *USS Theodore Roosevelt* (CVN-71) and the ship's carrier air group, the challenge was to show President Roosevelt's distinctive personality while maintaining the ship's identity. Roosevelt's big stick serves as the major prop. Compare this Aerocature™ with *In Defense of Freedom* (pages 34-35) and notice how the Navy's cast of airborne characters has dwindled.

11" x 14" Ink and Prismacolor® (1993)

air boss *noun* The yellow-shirt officer and veteran carrier pilot who is head of the air department on a carrier. The air boss is God when it comes to directing flight deck operations. With his second-in-command, the mini-boss, the air boss rules his dominion from on high in the ship's bridge.

yellow shirt *noun* The traffic cops of the flight deck. They coordinate all aircraft movement on a carrier in an incredible feat of choreography. Blasting jet exhausts, sucking air intakes, whirling propellers, and spinning rotor blades are hazards that go with the job.

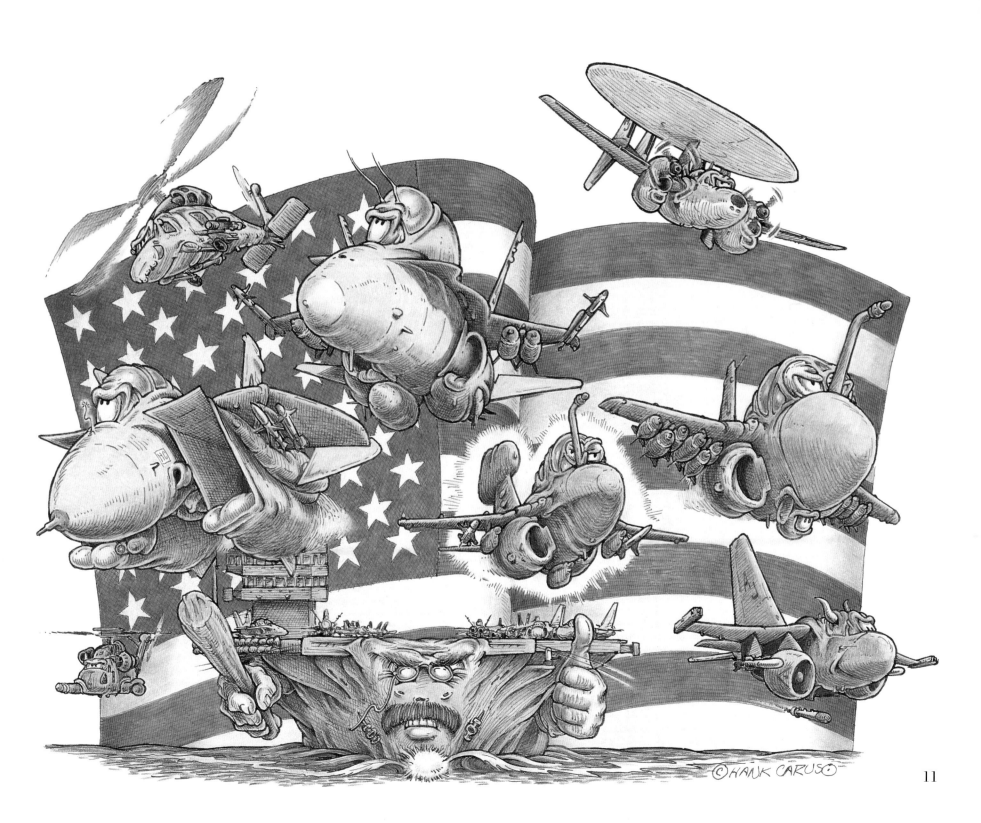

©HANK CARUSO

11

You Can Run But You Can't Hide

The Lockheed P-3 Orion first flew more than thirty-five years ago and its basic design remains unchanged today. It was designed at the height of the Cold War as a long-range patrol aircraft to counter the menace of Soviet submarines and their newly acquired capability to launch missiles from the sea. Over the years, its missions and capabilities have been expanded beyond its original sub-chasing role to include surface ship surveillance, electronic signal intelligence, and atmospheric research. The confrontation between Orion and Ivan was originally created for VP-65. It was one of my first professional Aerocatures™.

11" x 14" Ink (1982)

ASW *noun* Antisubmarine warfare. Here the Seabird sports the tools of the ASW trade: the can opener (mines, depth charges, and torpedoes) and the tail-mounted MAD boom (for detecting the distortions a submarine's metallic hull makes in the earth's magnetic field).

Bronco Bustin'

North American Rockwell's OV-10 Bronco made its first flight in 1965 in response to a tri-service requirement for a light armed reconnaissance aircraft. The Bronco was a highly versatile combat aircraft with a rear fuselage that was designed to carry cargo, armed troops, or casualties. The Marines and the Air Force were the primary users of this aircraft, although the Navy borrowed a few from the Marines for special river traffic interdiction during the Vietnam War. Later in its nineteen-year service life, the Bronco was used as a night observation gunship. This Aerocature™ shows a US Marine Bronco as it yanks and banks through the tree- and rock-lined skies down on the deck.

11" x 14" Ink (1987)

BB stacker *noun* Also known as red shirts or ordies (ordnance handlers). These enlisted ground crew keep the pointy end of Naval Aviation's spear sharp. They handle, load, and unload the bombs, guns, and missiles. Other red shirts defuse and disarm defective ordnance, fight fires, and operate crash and salvage equipment.

Pardon My Intrusion

The Grumman A-6 Intruder has been the premier Navy and Marine all-weather attack aircraft since its first combat use in 1965. Now it is leaving the active inventory as a result of post-Cold War force reductions. No other aircraft possesses its operational capabilities.

There is a distinct difference in attitude between attack and fighter pilots. Attack pilots just don't think that spending most of a mission flying straight and level at high altitude is really any fun. They prefer the challenge and sustained adrenaline rush of flying in constant close formation with the terrain. They believe that getting there and back should be at least as much fun as being there. This was certainly the attitude of Capt. Jeff "Chuck Wagon" Olsen (USMC) of VA-128 as we threaded our way through the Cascade Mountains in July 1990. As we banked over a pleasure boat on one of the mountain lakes, he exclaimed, "They were waving! I know they were waving! I love it when they wave!"

11" x 14" Ink and Prismacolor® (1985)

B/N noun Bombardier/navigator, the NFO of the Intruder cockpit team who operates the A-6 navigational and weapons systems. Also known as beaner. The unique side-by-side seating for the flight crew in the A-6 makes for an unusually high degree of coordination and partnership. Congratulatory high-fives are typical endings to successful strikes.

Grape Juice

The "dance" that takes place on the deck of an aircraft carrier is unmatched, either in complexity or danger, by any other military or civilian operation. It is truly a marvel of confidence and cooperation and I never get tired of watching it. While the dance is for the benefit of the aviators, it is the enlisted personnel who actually make it all work. Because the carrier deck is such a noisy and hazardous "office," flight deck personnel wear different colored jerseys to provide quick identification of who's who and who's doing what. Purple shirts, also known as grapes, are responsible for fueling and defueling aircraft.

11" x 14" Ink and Prismacolor® (1984)

blue shirt *noun* Aircraft-handling crew member and chockman. Blue shirts move the aircraft, operate aircraft elevators, and secure aircraft to the deck with wheel chocks and chains.

brown shirt *noun* Plane captain. Plane captains are responsible for the care, cleanliness, and general psychological well-being of the aircraft under their care.

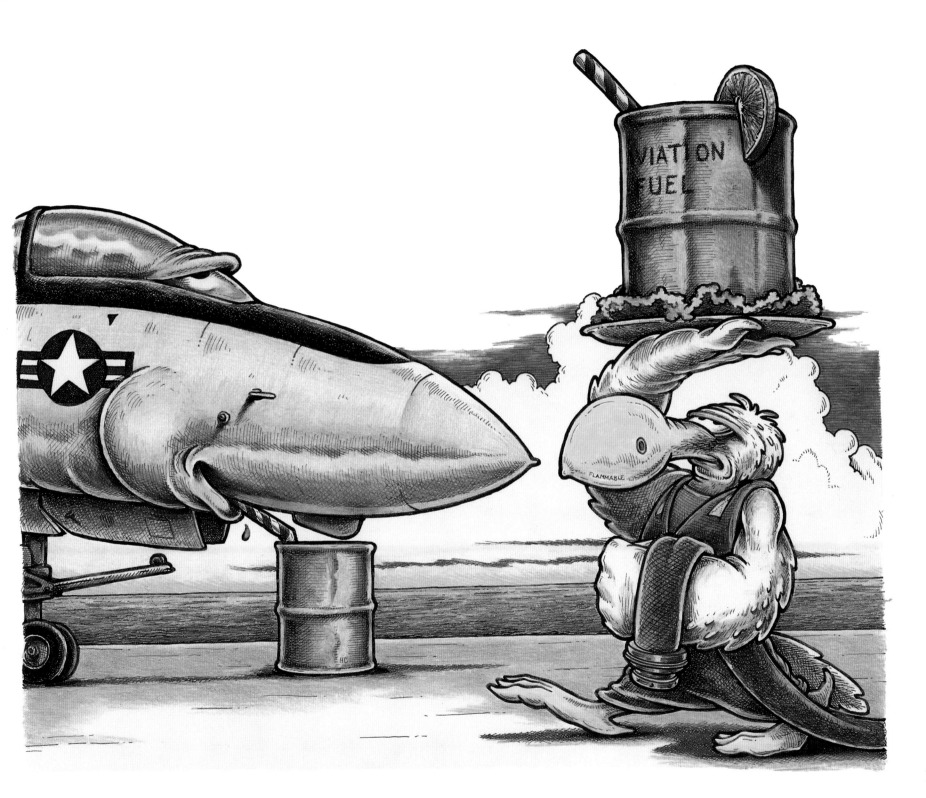

Cat Stroke Fever

Aircraft that operate from aircraft carriers are designed to withstand the incredibly punishing stresses of arrested landings and catapult launches. At a signal from the catapult officer (the shooter), a steam catapult accelerates an aircraft from a standing start to more than 160 MPH in less than three seconds. (I've been told that this is enough force to hurl a Cadillac more than a mile.) The massive nose gear strut on the McDonnell Douglas F/A-18 Hornet, which is typical of carrier aircraft, transfers the enormous forces of the cat shot from the carrier's launch shuttle to the aircraft frame.

During my first jet catapult launch (with LCdr. Barry Love in a TA-7 SLUF), my overloaded and disoriented senses told me that the back of the aircraft was being crushed against my back while the nose seemed to be getting further away in a grayish tunnel and driving down into the ground at the same time. Maybe it was.

14" x 22" Ink and Prismacolor® (1990)

cat *noun* **1.** A ship's catapult; **2.** A catapult launch, under the control of the yellow shirt, catapult officer, or shooter.

cat *verb* To launch an aircraft from a ship's catapult.

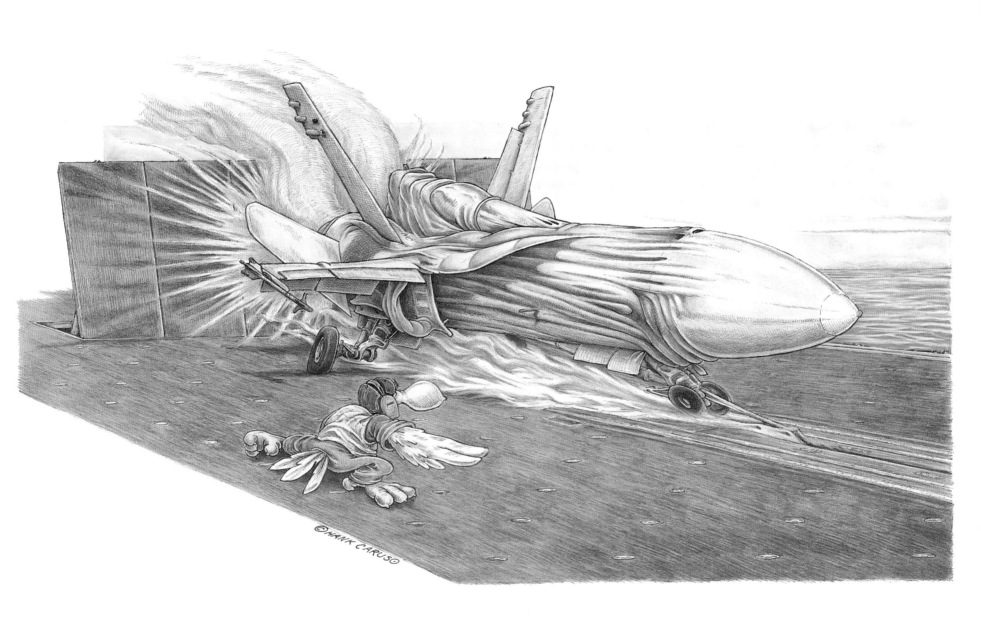

Medrider Farewell

The venerable Lockheed C-130 Hercules has served in many roles with the US Navy, Marines, Air Force, and the armed forces of numerous foreign countries. One of the more specialized roles that the Hercules fulfills is aerial refueling in the guise of the KC-130 tanker/transport. This illustration was commissioned to commemorate the disestablishment of the Navy's VR-22 Medriders in May 1993, leaving the Marines as the only operators of the Hercules in its tanker role. This Aerocature™ shows something that would not happen in real life: the simultaneous refueling of an F/A-18 Hornet and a CH-53E Sea Stallion. But to make the physics work out on paper, the Hornet is flying at a high angle of attack to slow it down and the Sea Stallion is in a slight dive to add speed. Then the Hercules banks towards the helicopter, thereby increasing the airspeed over the wing refueling the Hornet. Or at least that's the way it works in an Aerocature™.

11" x 14" Ink (1993)

COD *noun* **1.** Carrier on-board delivery. The delivery of critical priority shipments (movies and mail) and incidental cargo (personnel and supplies) to a carrier at sea; **2.** The aircraft that makes COD shipments.
COD *verb* To fly personnel and supplies or other materials to a carrier at sea.

Scratch One Bogey

The F-14 Tomcat flies the most impressive airshow demonstrations that I have ever seen. There are no perpendicular angles on the Tomcat, which contributes greatly to its dynamic image. It seems to be clawing its way through the air as it maneuvers. With a new, more powerful engine, the Grumman F-14A+ (since redesignated the F-14B) and F-14D Super Tomcat models remain worthy opponents for the latest generation of Soviet fighters, such as the Su-27 Flanker. The inspiration for this illustration was the thought of a Tomcat in an alley fight and the F-14's motto: "Anytime, baby!"

This was a difficult story to tell. I drew it at least three times. I wanted to clearly show a victor and a victim, but I did not want to depict the Flanker in such a way that the viewer would feel sorry for the loser. That would work against the humor of the overall image. I think the Flanker's cartoon violence wounds and puckered tailpipe succeed in giving the right feeling. The Russian woolly hat on the Flanker was a fun prop to use, but recent world events may have rendered it obsolete for future Aerocatures™.

14" x 22" Ink and Prismacolor® (1988)

debrief *verb* To determine the truth about what really happened during a mission or flight engagement. (Truth, of course, is defined by the person in possession of the chalk.)

debriefing *noun* A calm, dispassionate review of the lessons learned from a mission or flight engagement.

Surviving the Swim Test

Regardless of which aircraft he or she flies, no Naval Aviator escapes survival training. This training includes the dreaded survival swim, consisting of a seventy-five-yard swim and a fifteen-minute survival float. Unfortunately, these tests must be executed while the victim is dressed in a flight suit, steel-toed boots, G-suit, torso harness, survival vest, and helmet. All this gear weighs about forty pounds. But the real problem is not the weight, but rather how hard the water pushes back and how restricted body movement becomes.

When I finished this illustration, I had second thoughts. I was afraid it might be too much of an exaggeration. Then I looked at the photograph of me taken after I finished my swim test. I was completely exhausted and thoroughly waterlogged, inside and out. Maybe this illustration is an understatement.

8" x 11" Ink and Prismacolor® (1984)

dunker *noun* A device used to teach Naval Aviators how to escape from an aircraft that has found its way underwater. The helo dunker teaches blindfolded subjects how to escape from a submerged cabin in a calm and coordinated manner.

hypoxia *noun* A condition caused by oxygen deprivation. Altitude chambers acquaint aviators with the symptoms of hypoxia. At a simulated twenty-five-thousand-foot altitude without an oxygen mask, aviators observe changes in their coordination and awareness.

Jammin' Through the Waves

With all the offensive and defensive electronic systems arrayed against an attacking air force, a dedicated electronic equalizer is needed to clear a path through the electromagnetic waves that saturate the air. For the Navy, Marines, and Air Force, this equalizer is the Grumman EA-6B Prowler. A potent operational factor since 1972, the Prowler is based on the airframe of the A-6 Intruder. However, as I have been continually and forcefully reminded by the Prowler crews, they are not the same aircraft.

11" x 14" Ink (1987)

ECMO *noun* Electronic countermeasures officer. ECMOs assess the electromagnetic threats in the combat zone and determine what actions should be taken to evade and confuse the opponent's electronic sensors. Ultimately, ECMOs cast the Prowler's electromagnetic spell on the bad guys' radars to make the good guys invisible.

The Ambassadors

The US Navy's Flight Demonstration Squadron, also referred to as the "Ambassadors in Blue" or "Blue Angels," was established in 1946 to project a positive image for Naval Aviation through dramatic flight performances using the Navy's most capable tactical aircraft. When the team transitioned to the McDonnell Douglas F/A-18 Hornet in 1987, it adopted a most dramatic airshow performer.

I was privileged to fly with the team, under the command of Cdr. Pat Moneymaker, in March 1990. I was in the backseat of number four, the slot aircraft, flown by LCdr. Doug McClain. What was truly remarkable was not how close the team flies these aircraft to one another, but rather how unremarkable it all seems while it's happening. These pilots are so practiced and smooth that flying less than two feet apart at hundreds of miles per hour actually feels natural!

The most punishing part of flying with the diamond is not the show maneuvers themselves, but rather the hard turns that each aircraft makes following these maneuvers to clear show center for the solo pilots. During these turns, the G-meter routinely exceeds 7 Gs. The pilots don't wear G-suits (which they say get in the way) and neither did I. I managed to stay with the aircraft for the first three high-G excursions, but I literally fell asleep for a few seconds and started to dream during the fourth. I was feeling good until about an hour after the flight, during the debriefing. That's when my adrenaline quit pumping and my stomach finally faced reality.

14" x 22" Ink and Prismacolor® (1987)

Fat Albert *noun* The C-130 Hercules transport that provides logistical support for the Blue Angels. The C-130 is traditionally flown by a Marine Corps crew.

Semper Fly

The Marines have adopted a combination of aircraft developed for the US Navy and aircraft unique to the Marine inventory to accomplish their special close support missions. This family portrait of Marine aircraft includes the Grumman EA-6B Prowler, an aggressive radar jammer and despoiler, the venerable McDonnell Douglas A-4M Skyhawk attack aircraft, and the uniquely versatile McDonnell Douglas AV-8B Harrier.

11" x 14" Ink (1993)
From the private collection of Ed McGuigan, Jr.
Courtesy of Ed McGuigan, Jr.

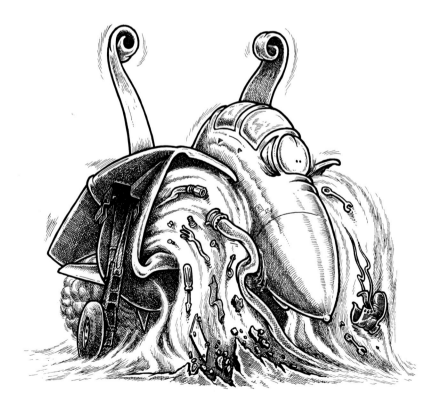

FOD *noun* **1.** Foreign object damage, generally used in reference to jet engines; **2.** Any object that could cause damage to an aircraft by being sucked into its engine or propelled by jet exhausts. Carrier deck crew perform a FOD walkdown at the beginning of each flight period to remove all potential FOD hazards.
FOD *verb* To cause foreign object damage to an engine or aircraft.

In Defense of Freedom

Created to commemorate the seventy-fifth anniversary of Naval Aviation, this Aerocature™ depicts a generic aircraft carrier air group, including most of the major aircraft types flown operationally within the past two decades. My goal here was to capture the resolve and determination that I've seen in the Navy and Marine aviators whom I've had the privilege of meeting in the past decade and a half.

Shown here (roughly in order of image size) are the F-14 Tomcat, A-6 Intruder, F/A-18 Hornet, S-3 Viking, F-4 Phantom II, E-2 Hawkeye, CH-46 Sea Knight, A-7 Corsair II, T-2 Buckeye, A-4 Skyhawk, F-8 Crusader, and SH-3 Sea King.

19" x 24" Ink and Prismacolor® (1985)

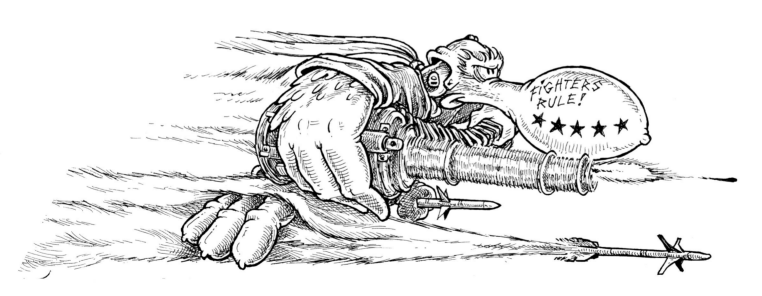

fox *exclamation* An aviator's announcement that a missile has been fired. "Fox one!" refers to firing a Sparrow missile, "Fox two!" a Sidewinder, and "Fox three!" a Phoenix (carried only by the F-14).

34

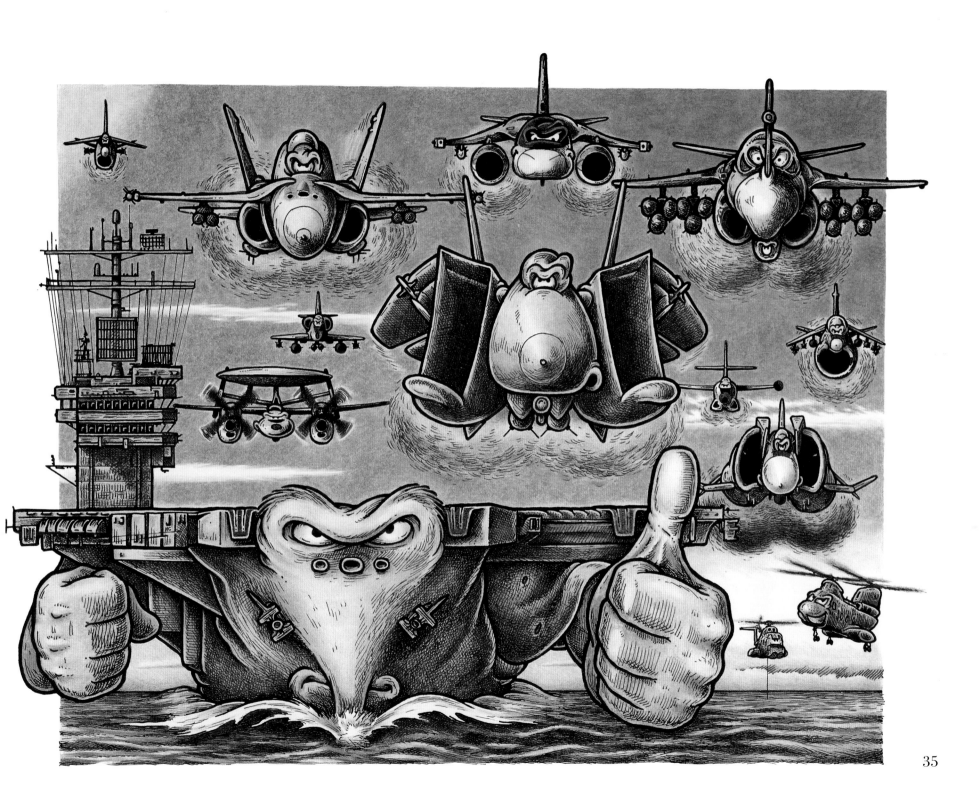

The Secret Life of G-Forces

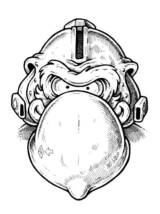 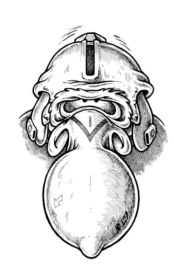 

Positive Gs *noun* Physical forces that act on pilots and aircraft during aerial maneuvers. Positive Gs push the aviator down into the seat. A couple of Gs are a piece of cake. A couple more Gs are still no sweat, even though they might be disorienting and may cause tunnel vision or a grayout. Lots of Gs (six or more) are another matter.

An aviator's blood pushes towards the feet and internal organs try to follow. Helmets become lead and oxygen masks and cheeks crawl down the aviator's face. Ultimately, the aviator may become a victim of a blackout or the potentially deadly G-LOC (G-induced loss of consciousness).

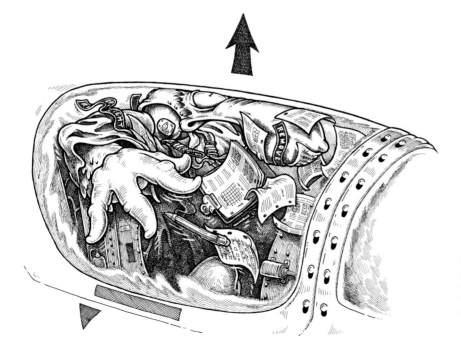

Negative Gs *noun* Negative Gs are much more uncomfortable and physically damaging than positive Gs. Negative Gs push the aviator's body up towards the canopy. The aviator's blood is pushed into the head, sometimes causing a redout or breaking blood vessels in the eyes. Because of the aviator's physical limitations, aircraft are also designed to withstand fewer negative Gs than positive Gs.

How Airplanes Fly

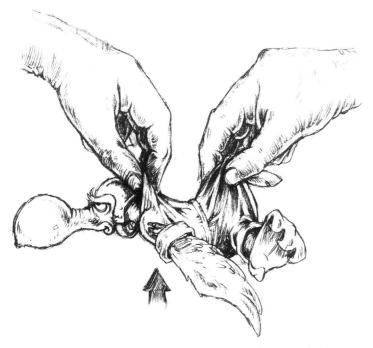

lifties *noun* Good physical forces that pull up on aircraft wings (also known as Bernoullies).

draggies *noun* Evil physical forces that oppose thrusties and try to slow down an aircraft.

thrusties *noun* Good physical forces that move an aircraft forward. Thrusties are produced by noise; the more noise an engine makes, the more thrusties it produces.

burner *noun* Afterburner. The tail end of a jet engine that causes a sudden onset of noise and thrusties.

School Days

Logic dictates that helicopters have no business being in the air. All that spinning metal and the precarious balance of dynamic forces that are the essence of rotary wing flight make these machines unlikely candidates for consistent, successful operations. But helicopters seem to work in spite of the odds stacked against them.

New pilots learn to confront the realities of rotary wing life in the Bell TH-57, the aerial classroom for the US Navy's student helicopter pilots. This Aerocature™ was commissioned by Helicopter Training Squadron Eight for its 1994 safety calendar. The fun part of creating this illustration was developing the training wheels image and all of the associated props that reinforce the idea of the rotationally prepubescent student's immaturity.

11" x 14" Ink (1993)

gouge *noun* Extremely important information, often not widely known, that is the ultimate embodiment of cosmic truth.
gouge *adjective* Deserving of a high degree of admiration or respect, as in "That's gouge!"

The Unsung

The glamor in Naval Aviation generally belongs to the officers, the pilots, and the NFOs, but there are many vital flight roles that are filled by enlisted personnel — the aircrew. This Aerocature™, originally created for *Naval Aviation News*, shows these roles.

Aircrew members serve as electronic systems operators on patrol and electronic jamming aircraft, such as the E-2 Hawkeye and EA-6B Prowler (top left). The loadmaster is responsible for managing cargo operations on the C-2 Greyhound and CH-53 Sea Stallion (top right). ASW (antisubmarine warfare) systems operators are key factors in the effectiveness of aircraft such as the P-3, S-3, and SH-3. The Seabird is shown here with a dipping sonar and a beak equipped with a magnetic anomaly detection (MAD) boom and ejector holes for sonobuoys (lower right). Life-saving search and rescue (SAR) swimmers jump from helicopters to aid downed aviators and others in distress on the sea (lower left).

14" x 22" Ink and Prismacolor® (1986)

A hand-picked ground crew keeps the Navy's Blue Angels on schedule for flight demonstrations throughout the year.

ground crew *noun* Indispensable enlisted personnel who toil in squadrons and on carriers around the world to keep Navy and Marine aircraft armed, available, and reliable. Red shirts, green shirts, and brown shirts are shown here.

Semper Torque

More than any other branch of service, the Marines rely on the versatility of rotary wing aircraft. Posing for this family portrait are (from left to right): Bell UH-1N Huey troop transport and medical evacuation helo; Bell AH-1W Cobra gunship; Sikorsky CH-53E Sea Stallion; Boeing Vertol CH-46 Sea Knight ("Frog"); Bell/Boeing V-22 Osprey (the Marines' next-generation assault, special operations, and strike rescue aircraft); and Lockheed KC-130 Hercules tanker/transport. (Okay, so the Hercules isn't really a helicopter. But propellers are sort of like rotors and torque — the power transferred from the engines to the rotors or propellers — is just as important.)

11" x 14" Ink and Prismacolor® (1994)

helo *noun* Helicopter, a flying machine that remains airborne by beating the air around it into submission. Some believe that continued intervention by the Almighty is also required. Helo crews acknowledge the religious aspects of rotary wing flight with their slogan, "To hover is divine."

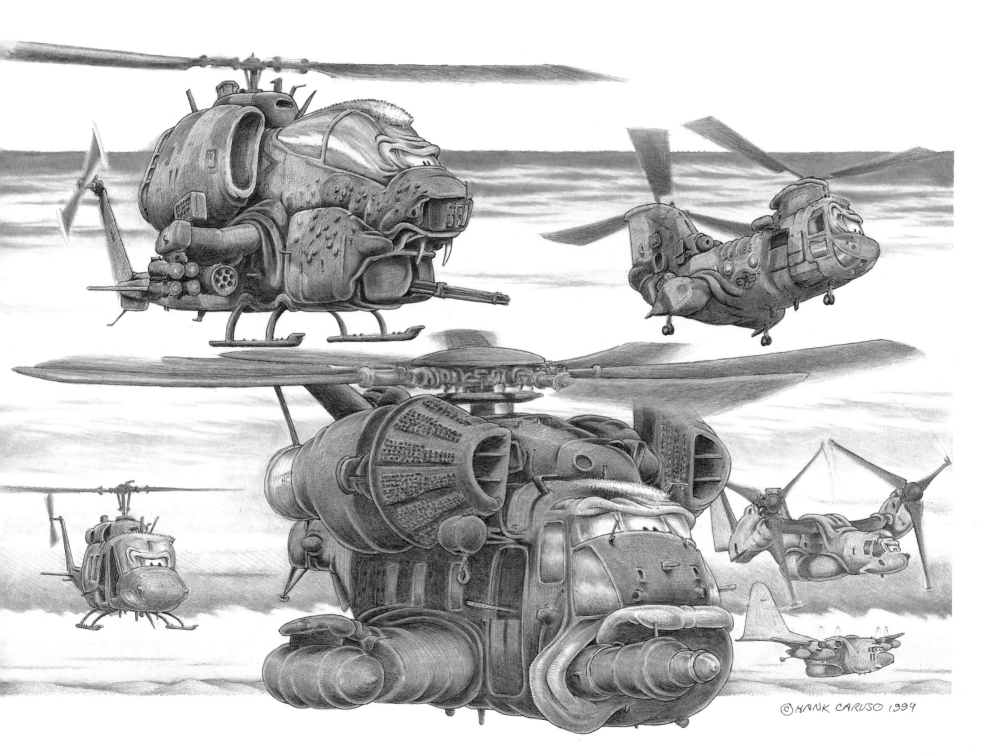

© HANK CARUSO 1994

43

Passing on the Spirit

It was formally known as the Corsair II, but everyone who flew or worked with the LTV A-7 called it the SLUF (Short Little Ugly F- - - - -). The A-7 was a scaled-down version of the Vought F-8 Crusader. Optimized for the ground attack role, the SLUF began its service career with the Vietnam War in the 1960s and left Navy operational service in 1991 after its last combat tour during Operation Desert Storm. This Aerocature™ was created to commemorate the disestablishment of VA-122. As it follows the A-1 Skyraider and A-4 Skyhawk attack aircraft into the history books, the legendary SLUF is shown passing on the spirit of light attack to its successor, the F/A-18 Hornet.

I am fortunate to have flown in the SLUF several times, including a catapult launch and an arrested landing. Most memorable was a low-level two-ship bombing exercise from NAS Patuxent River in which we rained twenty-five-pound "blue death" practice bombs on a decommissioned target ship off Bloodsworth Island. My pilot, Cdr. Bert "Professor" Johnston insisted that the pilots who had the real fun were the attack drivers. They fly on the deck to and from the target, work with the terrain, and always have scenery to look at close up. By the time we were done, I was willing to concede that the professor was right.

11" x 14" Ink and Prismacolor® (1991)

hernia bar *noun* A device used by red shirts (munitions handlers) to load bombs on aircraft when specialized bomb loading carts are not available.

Take a Deep Breath

Carrier Suitability (Carrier Suit for short) at NAS Patuxent River, Maryland, makes sure that the marriage of aircraft and carrier lives up to its vows. Aircraft carrier catapults produce massive clouds of steam that can rob aircraft of their "breath" and thrust. Here an LTV A-7 SLUF sucks in copious quantities of steam from Carrier Suit's TC-7 catapult facility to prove that it can still function properly in spite of its vaporous diet.

11" x 14" Ink and Prismacolor® (Naval Aviation News, May/June 1991)

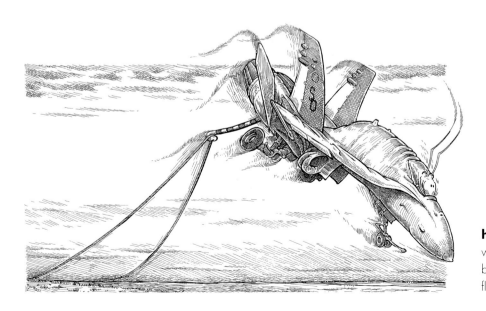

high trap *noun* The worst-case landing trial that an aircraft endures to prove it is worthy of carrier life. In a high trap, the tailhook of an aircraft snags an arresting wire before its main landing gear touches the deck. This punishingly abrupt end to normal flight is also known as an in-flight engagement.

©HANK CARUSO 1991

47

Jaws of the Ramp Monster

The birth of jet carrier aviation in the 1940s and 1950s was not an easy delivery. When the teething problems of early jet aircraft were combined with the remarkable demands of aircraft carrier operations, the result was probably the most difficult operating environment ever seen in the history of aviation. Initially, jet operations were conducted from straight-deck carriers. These carriers featured elevators in the middle of the flight deck and parked aircraft at the end of the very short landing area. Early jets were underpowered, and their engines were not responsive to rapid throttle changes, adding an extra element of risk to landing approaches. Training for flight crews operating on such ships was in its infancy. This combination of conditions was not conducive to a lengthy operational career.

This art was specially created for the Tailhook Association's Early Centurion certificate. This certificate commemorates those pioneering jet aviators who managed to keep themselves in one piece while accumulating one hundred or more traps (arrested landings) on straight-deck carriers. This was no trivial achievement. The title of this Aerocature™ was derived from the nickname given to the stern of the carrier, which devoured men and aircraft unlucky enough to find themselves behind the power curve on their landing approaches.

11" x 14" Ink (1990)

hook *noun* Tailhook. The device used by carrier-based aircraft to bring massive flying machines to a sudden stop (arrested landing) within a few hundred feet on a carrier deck.

hook *verb* To engage with a tailhook one of the thick cables (wires) strung across a carrier deck.

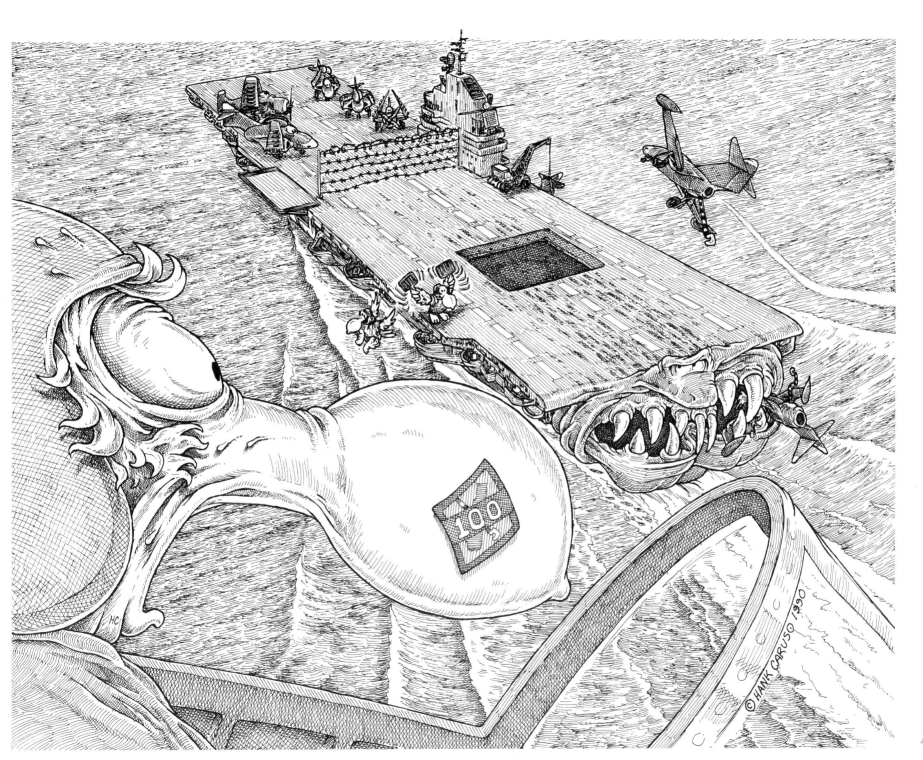

49

Adventures in Aero Medicine

Pilots and flight crew must be in excellent health to endure the rigors of military flying and to successfully complete a mission. Each aviator must pass a periodic flight medical examination. Knowing what's important to an aviator's health in high-performance flight comes from continued physiological research and data gathered on the ground and in the cockpit.

11" x 14" Ink and Prismacolor® (Approach, September 1988)

hot section inspection *noun* Jet engines must generate a continuous flow of noise to keep an aircraft flying. Green shirts on the ground ensure the health of each aircraft by continuous inspections and maintenance. Shown here is the critical hot section inspection.

gripe *noun* An electrical or mechanical problem with an aircraft. An "up" gripe means that it's still okay for the airplane to fly, but a "down" gripe grounds the aircraft until the problem is fixed.

Harrier's In Hot

The McDonnell Douglas AV-8B Harrier is unique in many respects, but it is primarily known for its ability to take off and land vertically. However, it's hard to show stationary hovering as a dynamic flight situation. Besides, it has little to do with the Harrier's actual ground attack mission. Therefore, I chose to show the Harrier in a high-speed attack run at low altitude, which better illustrates its personality as a combat warrior.

11" x 14" Ink and Prismacolor® (1986)

52

in hot *adjective* Refers to an aircraft that's approaching its target with its weapons armed and ready for release. A similar concept is "fangs out."

The Electronic Aggressors

Modern electronic systems are essential tools for today's military warrior. As a result, the air above the battlefield has become increasingly cluttered with electrons, both friendly and hostile. To survive and function effectively in this electromagnetic soup, air and surface systems operators must train in realistic simulations of the electronic battlefield. At the time this illustration was created, the electronic aggressors of VAQ-33 and VAQ-34 provided this essential training. Venerable Douglas ERA-3 Skywarriors (Whales) and Vought EA-7 SLUFs were used to simulate Soviet bombers and cruise missiles in mock attacks on Navy surface vessels to hone their crews' offensive and defensive skills.

Electromagnetic waves are invisible, so showing them in an illustration is a problem. In the ECM (electronic countermeasures) community, the lightning bolt and the crow serve as symbols of electromagnetic waves and the havoc they can wreak.

11" x 14" Ink (1988)

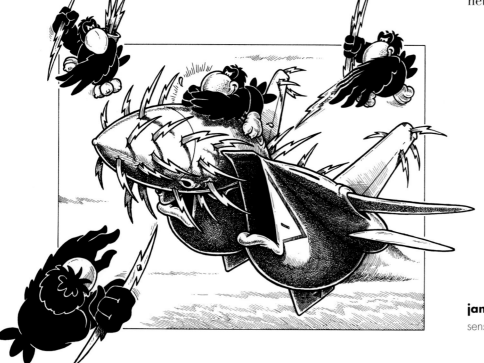

jam *verb* To confuse, blind, harass, misdirect, or otherwise molest an opponent's sensor systems, thereby avoiding detection or harm.

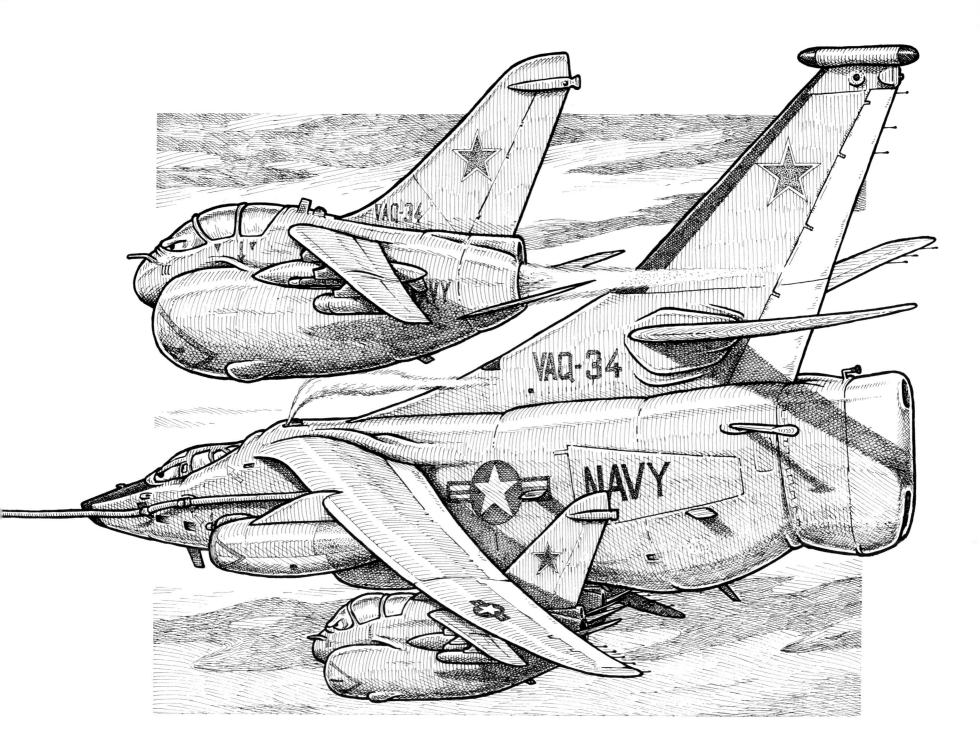

Shall Not Perish

The USS *Abraham Lincoln* (CVN-72) was the fifth Nimitz-class nuclear aircraft carrier to be commissioned. Its motto, "Shall not perish," is taken from President Lincoln's Gettysburg Address. The crew's sense of identity with the ship's namesake is strong on the "Abe," from the 1972 Lincoln-head penny that each crew member proudly wears on his name tag to the Lincoln profile that is ubiquitously displayed on bulkheads, panels, and equipment.

These Aerocatures™ were created for *Naval Aviation News* and are based on my impressions aboard the *Lincoln* during its initial aircraft/ship compatibility trials in November 1989. The illustration of Abe in the cockpit was inspired by the ship's first skipper, Capt. William Hayden, who added a stovepipe hat to his flight gear following his completion of the first official fleet trap aboard the *Lincoln*.

11" x 14" Ink (1992)

Workhorse with Wet Feet

One of the most impressive flying machines ever operated by the US military is the Sikorsky CH-53 Sea Stallion. Its power and size have made the Sea Stallion a fleet workhorse for nearly thirty years. The first time that I approached a powered-up Sea Stallion, I was pretty well mesmerized by the blurred momentum of the massive seven-bladed rotor spinning overhead and somewhat apprehensive about stepping any closer. Once inside the massive fuselage, the passage of the main rotor blades created pressure pulses against my chest that gave me an uncomfortable claustrophobic feeling for the first twenty minutes or so of flight.

This Aerocature™ shows the three-engined CH-53E model operated primarily by the Marines. The "cigar" clenched in the copter's jaw is the aerial refueling probe used to extend the Sea Stallion's range. The large semi-conical growths on the front of each engine are sand filters.

11" x 14" Ink and Prismacolor® (1984)

MCM *noun* Mine countermeasures. A variety of techniques for clearing mines from the seaways. These include the hydrofoil mine-sweeping sled shown here, which uses electromagnetic energy to detonate magnetically activated mines.

59

The Final Wake of the Whale

The Douglas A-3 Skywarrior was the largest aircraft ever to fly operationally from an aircraft carrier, hence its nickname: the Whale. Designed in the late 1940s at the beginning of the jet age and the Cold War, the Whale was the Navy's strategic delivery vehicle for primitive atomic weapons. It was retired from Navy operations in September 1991 after thirty-nine years of service in a variety of roles, including nuclear attack, aerial refueling, electronic intelligence, and electronic aggressor.

When VAQ-33 commissioned this Aerocature™, they wanted to show all of these different missions. We agreed that the primary visual emphasis should be on the original version of the Skywarrior, the A3D. The distant aircraft carriers are those on which the A3D completed its carrier suitability trials, the USS *Forrestal* (CVA-59) and the USS *Bon Homme Richard* (CVA-31). The deep blue color of the first few Whales was much more satisfying than its later low-visibility gray scheme. The Whale nickname is ideal for the A-3: the fluke-shaped wings and horizontal tail, and the ribbed underbelly were natural extensions of the aircraft's actual shape. The blowhole and water spout just seemed to go with the personality.

11" x 14" Ink and Prismacolor® (1991)

NFO *noun* Naval flight officer, an aviator who is an officer but not a pilot. Also referred to variously as backseater, 'FO, RIO, scope, grape, or mole. Many NFOs would have preferred to be pilots, but do not have good enough eyesight to fly. In the backseat, they are often the victims of motion sickness (note the bag) and unexpected violent maneuvers (note the pillows).

61

Trapping the Phantom

The McDonnell Douglas F-4 Phantom II is truly legendary in the annals of military aviation. First flown in 1958, the F4H-1, was developed by the Navy as its next generation multi-role fighter. The design was so superior that it was also grudgingly adopted by the Air Force (as the F-110). The version shown in this Aerocature™ is the F-4S, the last variant flown by the Navy and Marines. The F-4S was retired from Navy service in 1992.

Carrier landings are incredibly violent events. I wanted to show not just the act of landing but also to give a feel for the forces acting on the aircraft (as well as the flight crew). The beefy Navy landing gear compresses from the 5- to 6-G vertical deceleration. At the same time, the tailhook snags one of the cross-deck pendants (wires) so that the back of the plane comes to a stop while the rest of it tries to keep going forward.

11" x 14" Ink and Prismacolor® (1987)

no grade *adjective* The worst grade that a pilot can get for an arrested landing, indicating embarrassingly poor form or narrowly avoiding a serious mishap. (This sour-looking little character was the very first Seabird.)

Once Again Ensign Nolo Cheats Death

Even after the last active duty F-4 retired from Navy service, a few Phantoms flew on as missile target drones with the US Navy's Targets Directorate at NAS Pt. Mugu. These drone QF-4N Phantoms had a TV camera in the nose and a new flight control system so that they could be piloted from a remote location. When the QF-4N was used as a missile target, the mission was referred to as a NOLO (no live operator) flight. Otherwise, during practice or training missions, a safety pilot would be in the cockpit in case the remote control system or communications link malfunctioned. Each time a drone survived a missile firing, a missile escape silhouette was added to the intake splitter plate, a sort of reverse kill marking. The imaginary Ensign Nolo, piloting the unmanned drone, would also be promoted to the next rank.

The QF-4N in this illustration combines the Phantom's muscle plane characteristics and my pilot's personality. Ken "Bush" Bushpics was, at the time, a civilian pilot employed by the Targets Directorate. He was truly at home with the brute-force design of the Phantom, having grown up with the F-4 during the Vietnam era. He was as giddy as a school kid when we rolled out at altitude after the maximum performance takeoff from NAS Pt. Mugu that he arranged for us in October 1989. His black cowboy hat, Yosemite Sam moustache, constant cigarette, and Harley-Davidson motorcycle completed the image.

11" x 14" Ink (1989)

NOLO *adjective* No live operator. NOLO flights involve unmanned drone aircraft that are flown by pilots on the ground using remote control. The drone aircraft are equipped with TV cameras to give the pilot a tunnel vision view of what the drone aircraft "sees."

Tales of the Super Guppy

The Navy's primary jet trainer, the North American T-2 Buckeye, entered service more than thirty-five years ago in 1959. It is still in limited service today, having served as pilot and NFO trainer, spin trainer, weapons trainer, and aggressor. Its docile and forgiving nature makes it an ideal platform for student training. Only now is it being replaced by the McDonnell Douglas T-45 Goshawk.

My first hop in the Super Guppy was at NAS Pensacola in August 1984, when LCdr. Mike Rohman and the Cosmic Cats of VT-10 introduced me to the beauty and drama of basic aerobatics and formation flying. In contrast to the scenic route that I flew in Florida, my second flight was as a backseat observer for a spin training flight at the Naval Test Pilot School, NAS Patuxent River, in December 1985. With LCdr. Gray Morrison at the controls, I found out just how much my body mistrusts unusual flight attitudes. After the third spin, however, I think that I was beginning to accept the experience. Either that or I just ran out of adrenaline. Because of all that the T-2 has patiently endured, I chose to show it as the victim of considerable punishment at the hands of nugget pilots, bandaged and anticipating the worst.

11" x 14" Ink (1984)

nugget *noun* A neophyte aviator (pilot or NFO). Note the conscientious concern and benevolence of the God-like instructor pilot (IP).

The Lifeblood of Naval Aviation

The Naval Air Training Command is the birthplace of all Navy and Marine aviators. Over the years, it has used a number of different aircraft to train pilots and backseaters in their quest for aviators' wings of gold. This flyby of the USS *Lexington* tower was created for the cover of a special issue of *Naval Aviation News* devoted to the Naval Air Training Command.

Depicted in rough chronological order are the Curtiss N-9 (which became the Navy's standard seaplane trainer in 1916); Consolidated NY-2 Yellow Peril; Boeing-Stearman N2S-4; North American SNJ Texan (complete with greenhouse canopy); North American T-28 Trojan; Grumman TF-9J Cougar; Beech T-34C Mentor (upside-down); McDonnell Douglas TA-4J Skyhawk; North American T-2C Buckeye; Bell TH-57 Sea Ranger; and newcomer McDonnell Douglas T-45 Goshawk (replacement for the T-2). Of course, the ever-present Seabird maintains a watchful vigil over the students' progress.

14" x 21" Ink and Prismacolor® (Naval Aviation News, *July/August 1988*)

paddles *noun* Landing signal officer or LSO, a white shirt. The LSO keeps aircraft within the proper envelope for landing and waves them off (rejects them) if they stray outside safe limits. LSOs use radio calls instead of wielding the paddles they once used decades ago, but they still refer to their job as waving. The motto of the LSO school is "Rectum non bustus."

ball *noun* Meatball, the assembly of glideslope indicator lights (see paddles' beak) on the port side of the carrier that pilots use as a reference for landing. Pilots "call the ball" to confirm that they have these lights in sight.

Delivering the Hornet's Sting

The McDonnell Douglas F/A-18 Hornet and its flight crews have a large pair of shoes to fill: excelling in both the fighter and ground attack missions. Historically, these two roles have been separated by aircraft type and attitude. The Hornet relies on sophisticated electronic systems to give it the ability to fulfill both obligations. This means that the artist is also faced with the choice of which mode to portray. I chose the attack mode because there's something about the relation between the aircraft and the nearby ground during an attack mission that makes for a more dynamic image.

11" x 14" Ink and Prismacolor® (1985)
From the private collection of Carl Braun
Courtesy of Carl Braun

punch out *verb* To eject from an injured aircraft just before it decides to finish flying. A parachute descent, or nylon letdown, follows an ejection. A successful parachute deployment depends on the parachute rigger.

rigger *noun* Parachute rigger (aircrew survival equipment man), the Naval Aviator's guardian angel. The rigger is mechanic, electrician, tailor, seamstress, pyrotechnician, materials specialist, and shopkeeper all rolled into one.

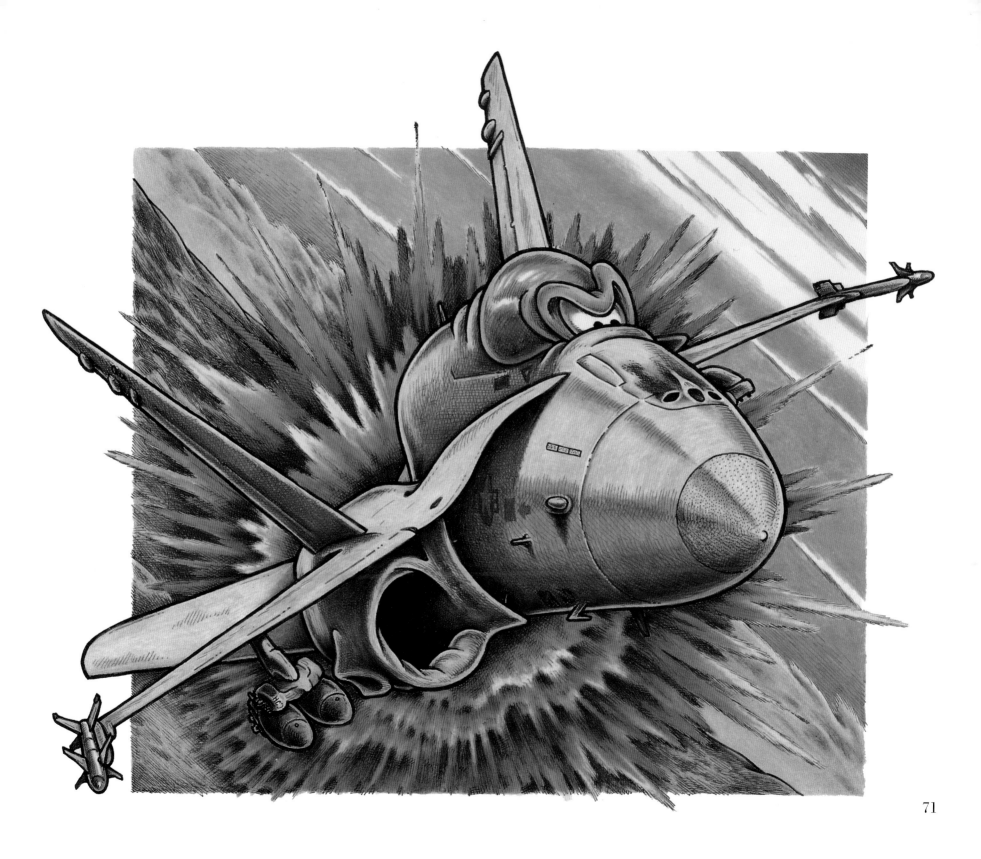

Take Charge and Move Out!

The expression "Take charge and move out" (TACAMO) describes the concept behind the Navy's airborne fleet communications broadcast system. A heavily modified Boeing 707 airliner, the E-6A Mercury is the first aircraft specifically designed for this mission. The Mercury uses dual trailing wire VLF antennas, which are several miles long, to maintain critical communications with submerged ballistic missile submarines around the world. The trailing wires are deployed while the aircraft is in a steep angle of bank so that the end of the antenna remains in a fixed location over the water.

This Aerocature™ was created especially for the flight crews of VQ-3, the first squadron to fly the E-6A. A sister squadron, VQ-4, also operates the Mercury. The name Mercury was selected since the aircraft's namesake was the messenger for the ancient Roman gods. The winged heels generally depicted on images of the mythological character were the inspiration for the small wings on the E-6A engines.

11" x 14" Ink and Prismacolor® (1994)

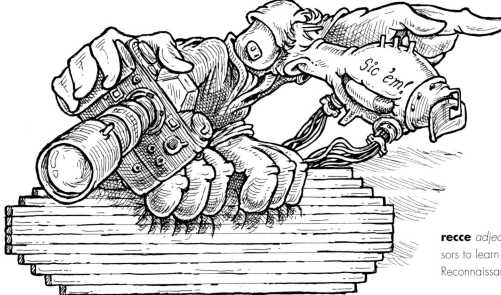

recce *adjective* Reconnaissance. Reconnaissance aircraft carry different kinds of sensors to learn as much as possible about an opponent's forces and capabilities. Reconnaissance sensors include cameras, infrared, and radar systems.

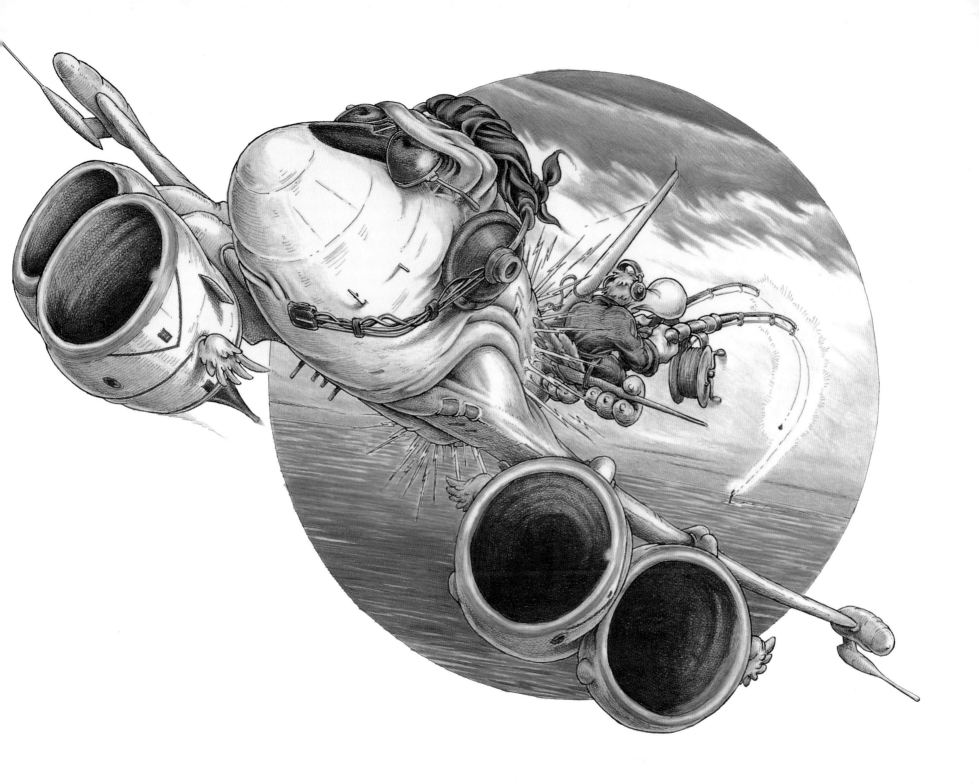

The Last Round-Up

The Sikorsky SH-3 Sea King has been in active Navy service since 1961. Its primary missions have been antisubmarine warfare (ASW) and search and rescue (SAR). It is now being replaced by the Sikorsky SH-60. This Aerocature™ was created for the Sea Griffins of HS-9 to commemorate the disestablishment of the squadron in 1993. The illustration reflects the cowboy image that the squadron wanted to portray, including cowboy hat, tail wheel spur, and lasso. The armed door gunner, homing torpedo, and night vision goggles reflect the expansion of the Sea King's operational role in recent times.

11" x 14" Ink (1993)

SAR *adjective* Search and rescue. A rescue helicopter is referred to as a SAR Bird.

Red Sail's in the Sunset

The Lockheed S-3 Viking began life in 1972 as a dedicated ASW (antisubmarine warfare) aircraft to protect the carrier battle group from undersea threats wherever it went. In recent years, the S-3 has assumed new roles under the heading of force warfare, which includes sea surveillance, mine patrol, surface combat air patrols, and scout reconnaissance as well as the original ASW role. The S-3 is also used for aerial refueling and has been modified into a special variant, the ES-3, for electronic intelligence.

My first flight in a Navy tactical aircraft was in an S-3A from VS Wing One at NAS Cecil Field with LCdr. Tom Linthicum at the controls. I was surprised at the nimble maneuverability of the Hoover. (The nickname comes from the unique sucking whoop made by its high-bypass turbofan engines.) This Aerocature™ shows a Soviet submarine being surprised on the surface by an S-3B loaded with Harpoon missiles. This is an unlikely operational situation, but is allowed under the caricaturist's license. The title is a play on words using an old song title and the fact that the vertical structure on submarines is called a sail.

11" x 14" Ink and Prismacolor® (1985)
From the private collection of Ralph Alderson
Courtesy of Ralph Alderson

senso, tacco *noun* Sensor operator and tactical coordinator. The P-3 and S-3 aircrew members who gather and analyze data from acoustic, electromagnetic, and infrared sensors. This information is used to identify and pursue submarines and other potential targets.

At the Merge

Some of the most critical decisions for a fighter pilot must be made at the merge, the point at which all of the combatants merge into one indeterminate blob on the tracking radars. Short of actual combat, the most realistic training for these situations comes from flying against the Aggressor squadrons of the US Navy and Air Force. At the time this illustration was done for the Challengers of VF-43, the Aggressors flew a variety of aircraft, including the Northrop F-5 Tiger, General Dynamics F-16N Fighting Falcon, and the Douglas A-4 Skyhawk, to provide pilots with experience in dissimilar combat (combat between aircraft of different capabilities). Substituting experience and superior tactics for aircraft sophistication, the Aggressors still manage to water the eyes of students who fly more capable aircraft, such as the F-14 Tomcat.

11" x 14" Ink (1990)

78

situational awareness (SA) *noun* An understanding of what's going on, having a clue. Losing an aerial engagement is often the result of losing situational awareness.

Escort Service

One mission of the F-14 Tomcat is to guard the outer perimeter of the battle group and ensure that intruders are looked after appropriately. This includes escorting potential threats, such as the burly Soviet Tu-95 Bear, away from the friendlies on the surface. I chose VF-143, the Pukin' Dogs, as the subject of this illustration because of the wonderful rudeness of the name and the image.

The squadron's emblem was originally supposed to be a winged panther. According to squadron legend, when the new design was first unveiled in 1958, the skipper's wife observed that it looked more like a puking dog than a mythological beast. The name stuck.

11" x 14" Ink and Prismacolor® (1984)

six o'clock *noun* The position directly behind an aircraft, also referred to as a pilot's six, as in "Check your six!" Shown here is the six-o'clock view that an attacker hopes his opponent sees.

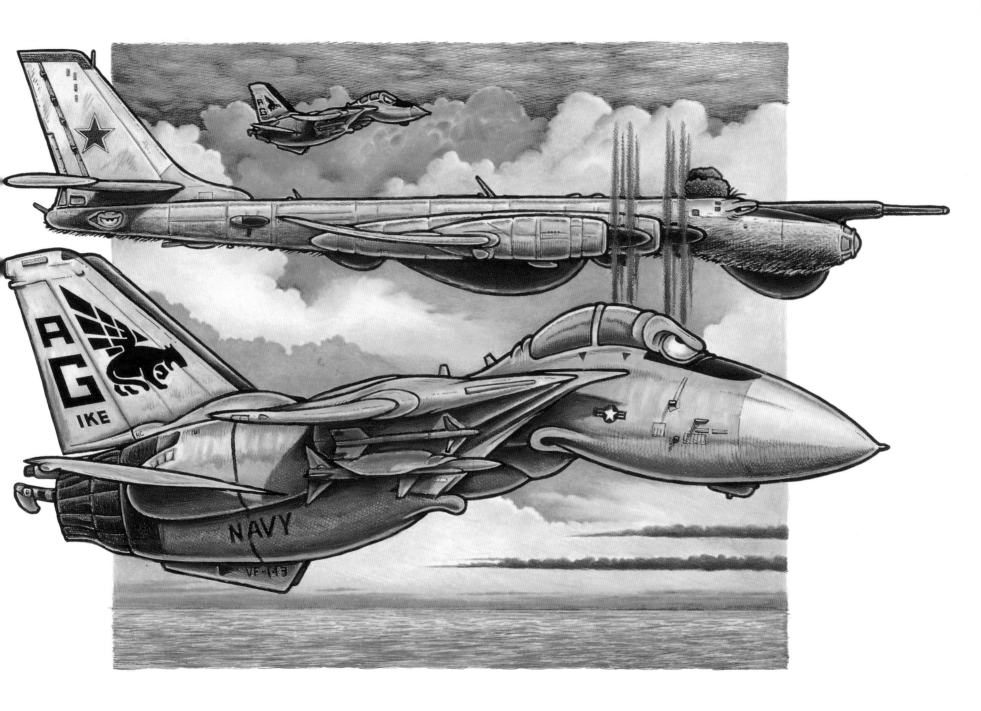

Scooters

The diminutive Douglas A-4 Skyhawk has a pugnacious personality all its own. It was first flown in 1954 in the early days of the jet age. Legendary designer Ed Heinemann defied the belief that new aircraft had to be progressively bigger, heavier, and more expensive. As a result of Heinemann's success in achieving his goal, the A-4 was popularly (and affectionately) known as Heinemann's Hot Rod, Scooter, and Tinker Toy. The versatile and long-lived design served the Navy and Marines in a wide variety of roles including attack, trainer, aggressor, target tow, and showbird with the Blue Angels Flight Demonstration Squadron.

My Skyhawk backseat experience was a VIP flight in Blue Angels #7 TA-4 with LCdr. Curt Watson in August 1984. LCdr. Watson proceeded to demonstrate the nimble maneuvering qualities that made the A-4 such a sparkling airshow performer. This was my first exposure to anything more acrobatic than a sixty-degree bank. We went through an entire series of acrobatic maneuvers including loops, rolls, Immelmanns, Cuban eights, and a series called the Squirrel Cage. The A-4 had an eye-watering roll rate of 720 degrees per second, but I couldn't manage to coax anywhere near that performance from the plane when I tried my hand at the stick.

11" x 14" Ink and Prismacolor® (1993)

stick *noun* **1.** A pilot. With "hot," an outstanding pilot, as in a "hot stick." **2.** The control apparatus used to control the position and appearance of the ground with respect to the aircraft. For example, pushing the stick forward makes trees and houses get bigger.

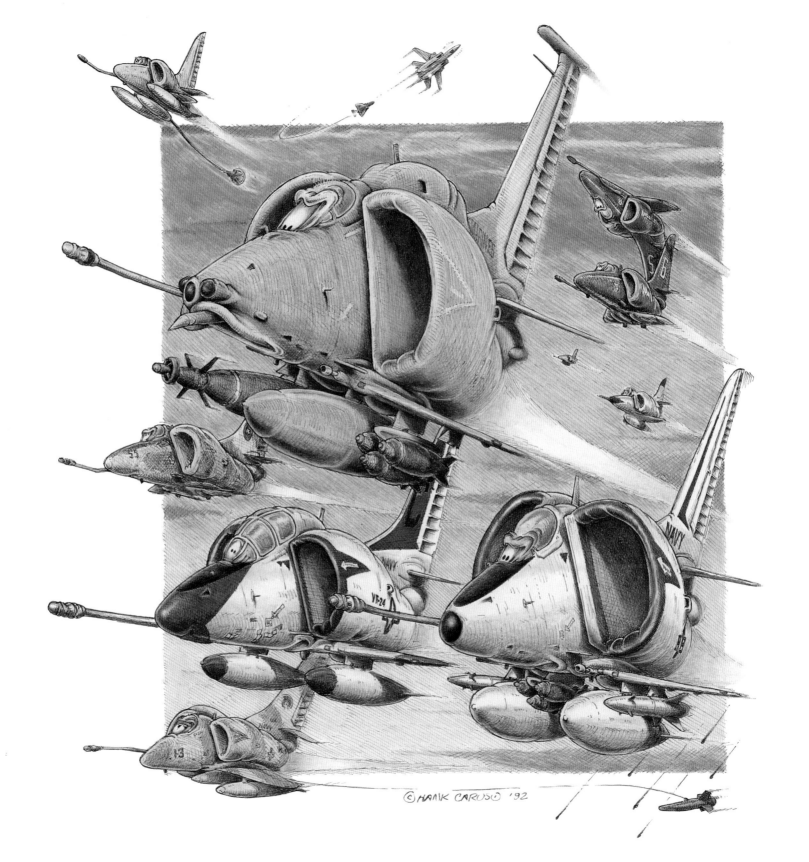

© HANK CARUSO '92

83

Test Pilots Then and Now

1945 — When the first US Naval Test Pilot School (USNTPS) class convened on 12 March 1945, the jet age was beginning to push the boundaries of flight to incredible extremes and new aircraft were not completely sure how they should behave in the air. Cockpit quarters were cramped and instrumentation was primitive. Early test pilots and test pilot students were often hard-charging combat veterans whose seat-of-the-pants flying habits had to be systematically untaught.

The need to look good for surprise photo opportunities made the cigar a critical piece of flight gear. Helmet scuffs on the tight-fitting canopies documented the flight envelope of the backseater's head. To make aircraft fly faster, test aircraft were adorned with large areas of red paint. Aerodynamicists refer to this phenomenon as chromakinetic augmentation.

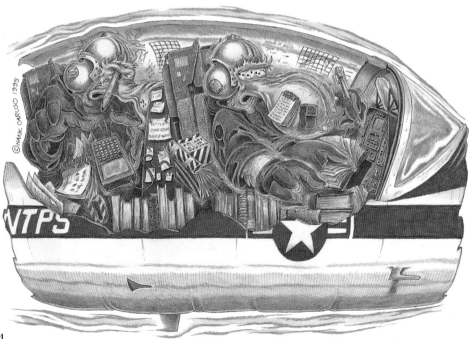

1995 — Today, test flying, as well as learning to be a test pilot, is a highly disciplined process. The cockpit is combination flying test laboratory and classroom. Nibbling at the edges of the flight envelope in small, carefully defined bites may disappoint many because it's so . . . boring.

The unglamorous reality of most test flying today is a gift from previous generations of test pilots, who devoted their careers, and sometimes their lives, to removing the uncertainty and unwarranted risk from their profession. While religious experiences in the cockpit are still a fact of life, the balance has shifted towards rediscovering the known rather than being compromised by the unknown.

1945 ⋆ USNTPS 1995

Pushing the Envelope

The US Naval Test Pilot School (USNTPS) trains Navy and Marine pilots and engineers as well as all US Army helicopter test pilots. In fifty years of operation, the USNTPS training syllabus has included nearly sixty different aircraft types. This flyby, commemorating the fiftieth anniversary of the USNTPS, shows about half of the aircraft types the school has flown.

14" x 22" Ink and Prismacolor® (Naval Aviation News, May/June 1995)

1 PBY-6A, **2** FM-2, **3** F4U-4, **4** SH-34G, **5** FJF-3, **6** F9F-5, **7** T-1A, **8** S-2A, **9** UH-1E, **10** OV-1A, **11** TF-8A, **12** F4D-1, **13** C-54Q, **14** NU-1B, **15** AD-5N, **16** CH-46E, **17** T-39A, **18** T-28B, **19** TA-4F, **20** TA-7C, **21** OH-61, **22** T-2C, **23** U-6A, **24** UH-60, **25** T-38, **26** X-26A, **27** F/A-18B, **28** AH-1G, and **29** P-3.

Another Lesson Learned at Top Gun

The US Navy's Fighter Weapons School, popularly known as Top Gun, gives fighter pilots and their backseaters as realistic a taste of actual air-to-air combat as possible before they are committed to action in a real war. Top Gun aircraft, such as the Northrop F-5 Tiger II, allow Top Gun students to fly against aircraft with different performance characteristics than their own aircraft. The F-5 was used because it was a good approximation of the MiG-21.

My introduction to Top Gun flight operations was courtesy of Lt. Sandy "Jaws" Winnefeld, a Top Gun instructor. The wings of the F-5 are so small that they really don't seem capable of providing any useful lift. Nevertheless, the F-5 is a hot rod, small and nimble, an excellent aircraft for the Top Gun mission. The highlight of our flight was a manhood-expanding trip through the sound barrier (in a shallow dive, to conserve fuel). After pulling out of the dive, we pushed over in an extremely disorienting zero-G recovery at the top of the climb. Even though my eyes told me we were right side up, my body was convinced that we were upside down. Throughout the flight, my ill-fitting helmet put strong pressure on the base of my skull. My stomach wasn't too happy with the rubber smell from my oxygen mask either. As a result, my body's endurance dropped rapidly towards the end of the flight.

11" x 14" Ink and Prismacolor® (1983)

Top Gun *noun* The US Navy's Fighter Weapons School. Contrary to the popular myth created by the movie of the same name, Top Gun is a rigorous educational institution, not a race for a prize. Instructors are chosen not only for their flying skills, but—equally as important—for their communication skills in the classroom.

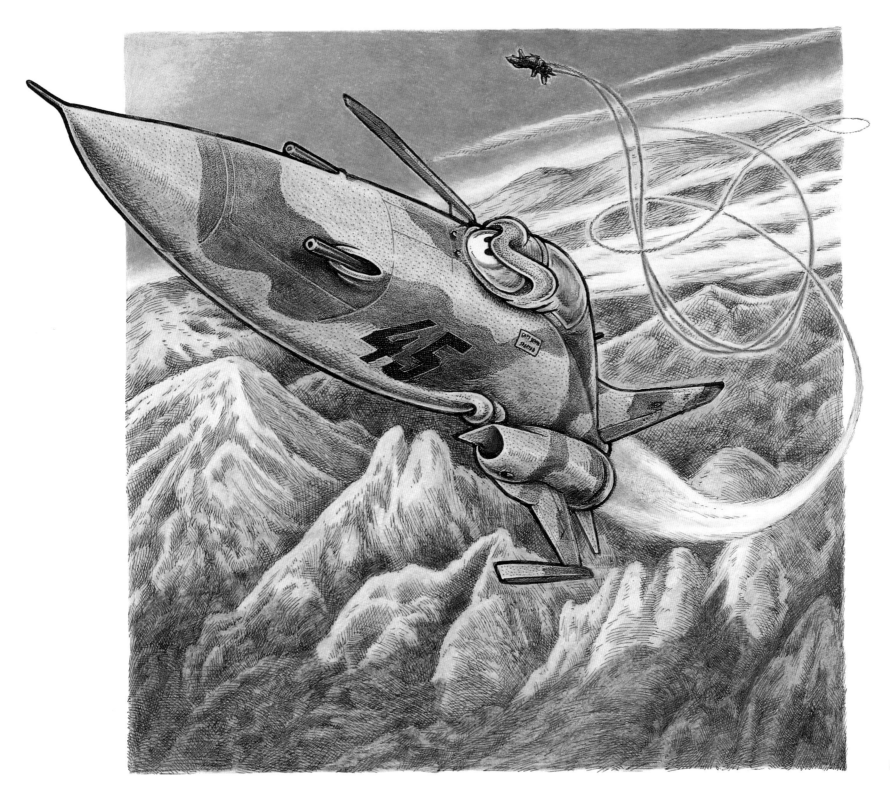

Hookin' a Hawkeye

The Grumman E-2C Hawkeye, or "Hummer," represents the farthest looking eyes of the fleet. This radar patrol aircraft provides early warning of possible threats to the carrier battle group and coordinates aircraft interceptions. The Hawkeye's most distinctive feature is its twenty-four-foot diameter radar dome that constantly rotates to scan the skies for unwelcome intruders. Its eighty-foot wingspan (like that of its structural cousin, the C-2 Greyhound) leaves its pilots almost no margin for error when landing within the narrow confines of a carrier deck.

Carrier landings are incredibly stressful events for pilots. Instrumented pilots making night carrier landings have shown higher levels of stress than any other profession. As I sat in the back seat of a TA-7 SLUF approaching the land-based arresting gear facility at NAS Patuxent River, the hot mike between me and the front seat made it obvious just how task-fixated a pilot becomes during a carrier approach. Cdr. Bob Christensen's breathing became dramatically louder and faster as our rapidly descending aircraft drew closer and closer to the arresting wire stretched across the runway.

11" x 14" Ink (1984)

trap *noun* An arrested landing aboard an aircraft carrier. High numbers of traps indicate exceptional worthiness and are advertised on flight jacket patches.

trap *verb* To complete an arrested landing aboard a carrier.

88

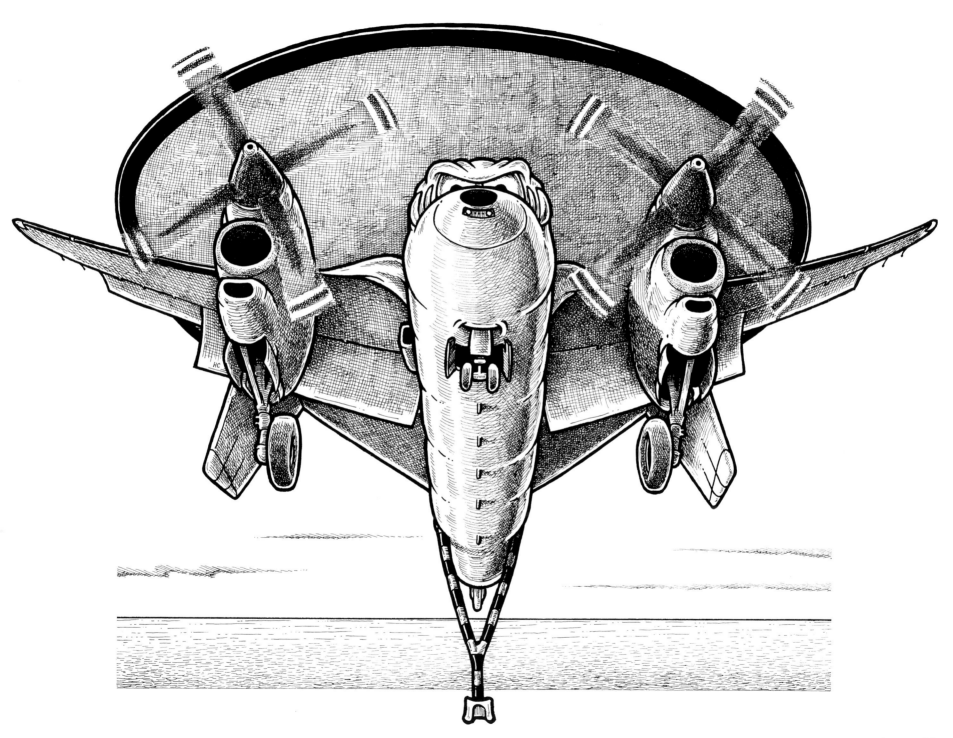

Seascrape

Named for the shield of Zeus in Greek mythology, the Aegis guided missile cruiser is a modern-day shield for the US Navy. It is the command and control nucleus of a complex weapons system network that involves both aircraft and surface ships. This network provides fleet defenses for countering surface and air threats. This Aerocature™ shows the Ticonderoga-class cruiser *Valley Forge* (CG-50) as it directs a hypothetical air battle involving the F-14 Tomcat and F/A-18 Hornet. I like using the image of eyes as representations of radar functions, even though eyeballs and radars use different parts of the electromagnetic spectrum. Fortunately, I don't have to contend with too many critics who are electromagnetic specialists.

11" x 14" Ink and Prismacolor® (1988)

trons *noun* Electrons. Sorting out the sometimes perverse behavior of trons in aircraft electronics is one of the jobs assigned to the green shirts. Other green shirt deck crew responsibilities include operating the ship's powerful catapults and rugged arresting gear.

Frog Legs

Boeing Vertol's CH-46 Sea Knight has served the Navy and Marines for more than thirty years, but no one ever calls it by its proper name. To its crews, the CH-46 is the Frog because of how it looks while it's squatting on the ground. The Frog is used primarily for search and rescue operations and underway replenishment (unrep) of vital supplies for ships at sea. Its versatility and maneuverability make it ideal for these roles. I've spent many hours marveling at the flying skill of CH-46 pilots as they crisply and precisely bring their aircraft to a brief hover over the ship's deck to pick up or release cargo.

When I flew the Frog from the carrier back to shore, two things caught my attention. First, those wonderful bubble windows on the fuselage gave me a great view. I could cram my head far enough into the window to look straight forward and back along the aircraft. The other was the distinct feeling that the aircraft didn't know which of its two rotors was supposed to be in front. There is something about the way the Frog moves in flight that made me feel as if it were constantly trying to swap its front and back ends. As a result, I came away with an even greater respect for the flying skills of the Frog pilots whom I watched during those long cargo exercises at sea.

11" x 14" Ink (1985)

vertrep *noun* Vertical replenishment. An act by which helicopters shuttle many tons of supplies and munitions from one ship to another.

Lady Lex

In November 1991, the USS *Lexington* (AVT-16) (a.k.a. the Lex or Blue Ghost) was decommissioned, ending more than twenty-two years of service as the Navy's training aircraft carrier. During this time, thousands of new flyers completed the first arrested landings and catapult launches of their careers on board the Lex. These rites of passage for all Naval Aviators are known as carrier qualifications, or carquals.

This image is undoubtedly the single most recognized Aerocature™. When I was asked by *Naval Aviation News* to create a cover for its 1983 Air Training Command issue, I had never drawn a carrier before. Nor had I ever been on or even near one. Therefore, I was really not prepared for the overwhelmingly enthusiastic reaction that I received from the Naval Aviation community, especially the telephone call from RAdm. Pete Booth (then chief of Naval Air Training, CNATRA) inviting me aboard the Lex for a familiarization cruise. This opportunity eventually made it possible for me to fly backseat in many different Navy aircraft.

Years later, I received a telephone call from one of the arresting gear operators on the Lex. He called my attention to the baseball glove at the back of the carrier and said proudly, "See that catcher's mitt? That's me!"

11" x 16" Ink and Prismacolor® (Naval Aviation News, September/October 1983)

wire *noun* One of four 1 1/2-inch thick arresting cables (cross-deck pendants) strung across the landing area of a carrier deck. The third wire from the stern of the carrier (the three-wire) is the ideal target for each arrested landing. The best grade that a pilot can earn for a carrier landing is an <u>OK-3</u>.

96